SPORTY SCRAPPIN'

snappy snippets that score

SPORTY SCRAPPIN'

snappy snippets that score

Jennifer Smith

Bluegrass
Publishing

www.bluegrasspublishing.com

For information contact:
Bluegrass Publishing Inc.
PO Box 634
Mayfield, KY 42066 USA
Phone: 270.251.3600
service@bluegrasspublishing.com
www.bluegrasspublishing.com

ISBN: 978-1-59978-006-1

1st. ed.
Mayfield, KY: Bluegrass Publishing Inc., 2007

Cover Design: Kevin Massiglia

Proudly printed in the United States of America

Table of Contents

Table of Contents

Table of Contents

Table of Contents

Dedication

First of all, I want to praise the good Lord, and thank Him for blessing me. My mama always told me that when God closes one door, He opens so many more, and boy, was she right. God put me in the place He wanted me, in order to give me the means to be able to support my boys. Thank you, Lord!

To my boys-Jordan and Andrew. I love you both so very much. It's hard to believe that you can love someone as much as I love you two. You are my angels. God sent you special to me, and I thank Him everyday for sending you two to me. You two are the reason I get up every morning. I cannot imagine my life without you in it. If it weren't for you two, I wouldn't have had the need for this book. You are my inspiration. You are the reason I breathe. You are the reason my life goes on. I love you both with all my heart. You two are such wonderful young men. I pray everyday that you two will grow up to be good men. I never dreamed that you two could be as awesome as you already are. I am so proud of you, and I am so proud that I am your mom.

Mama and Daddy, remember when I was little? I was a terror. I bet you never thought I would ever grow up and learn to appreciate you two. Well... I know now just how blessed I am to have parents like you. Not only do you support me in whatever I choose to do, you also love me no matter what. We've all been through a lot and its taken me a very long time to grow up, but I couldn't have done it without your constant love and prayer. Thank you for never giving up on me, and for loving me and my boys.

Missy, Jon, and Alan-I know I can be a brat, but I do love you and thank you for helping me and supporting me. Thank you for loving my boys.

Mari Jane-I really don't have to write anything here for you, because you already know what's on my mind. I know we're cousins, but to me, you're my very best friend. You're my confidant, my cheerleader, and my psychologist. Thank you for loving me. Thank you for accepting me for who I am, and encouraging me to be me. Thank you for never giving up on me. Thank you for listening to me cry for hours and hours. You are the only person in this whole world who truly understands me, yet, you still love me. How did I get so lucky? When I grow up, I wanna be just like you!!!

Grandma Annie, Aunt Dorothy, Uncle Tommy, Aunt Betty, Uncle, and all my other family members-I love you!!! Thank you for all your prayers.

Linda, Dorothy, and Bethany-you guys are awesome. Thank you for believing in me and supporting me.

Archery

- A Bolt from the Blue
- Absolutely Fletching
- Artful Archer
- Bull's-eye!
- Don't Want to Show You Up
- Eat Your Heart Out, Robin Hood!
- I Left My Arrows at Home
- I wasn't Aiming for the Target!
- My Quiver's Full
- Point Blank
- Practice Makes Perfect
- Slipped on the Grass
- Shoot for the Moon
- So Close!
- Straight as an Arrow
- Straight Shooter
- Sun Got in My Eyes
- Take a Bow
- That Arrow Has been Flying Funny All Day
- William Tell I ain't!
- The history of the bow and arrow is the history of mankind. ~ Fred Bear
- Old archers never die, they just bow and quiver.
- If you would hit the mark, you must aim a little above it; every arrow that flies feels the attraction of earth. ~ Longfellow
- There is no excellence in archery without great labor. ~ Maurice Thompson
- I shot an arrow into the air. It fell to earth, I knew not where. ~ Longfellow
- True archers make the competition quiver.
- I shoot an arrow into the air, where it lands I do not care: I get my arrows wholesale! ~ Curly Howard
- The more obstinately you try to learn how to shoot the arrow for the sake of hitting the goal, the less you will succeed in the one and the further the other will recede. ~ Eugen Herrigel
- Man, did you see how fast that arrow flew past the target?
- So long as the new moon returns in heaven a bent, beautiful bow, so long will the fascination of archery keep hold in the hearts of men. ~ Maurice Thompson
- Walk softly, but carry a big stickbow.

13

- When an archer misses the mark, he turns and looks for fault within himself. Failure to hit the bull's-eye is never the fault of the target. To improve your aim—improve yourself.
  ~ Gilbert Arland

- If you can shoot only one arrow a day, but concentrate with full focus on that one arrow, I believe it will do you more good than shooting 100 arrows. ~ Bryon Ferguson

Automobile Racing

- A 10-Car Pileup Never Happens Behind You!
- Along for the Ride
- And the Winner is...
- And They're Off!
- At the Track
- Away He Goes
- Back on Track
- Beat the Clock
- Black Flag—All Stop—Bad Accident
- Born to Race
- Breaking Away
- Breakneck Speed
- Bumpin', Crunchin' & Draftin'

- Burning Rubber
- By a Length
- Can't Wait to Get on the Road Again
- Caution—Yellow Flag
- The Checkered Flag
- The Competition
- A Day at the Races
- Driver Wanted
- The Driver's Seat
- Driving Force
- Easy Rider
- Enjoying the Ride
- Fast, Faster, Fastest
- A Fighting Chance
- Final Circuit
- The Finish Line
- Four on the Floor
- Friends Don't Let Friends Apex Early
- Full Throttle
- Garage Guru
- Gentlemen, Start Your Engines!
- Go Fast! Turn Left!
- GO GO GO!
- Going in Circles
- Going the Distance

- Good Timin'
- Good to Go
- The Green Flag
- Green, Green, Green!
- Green Means Go!
- Hairpin Turns
- He's Kissin' The Wall
- High Anxiety
- High Hopes
- Hot Wheels
- I Drive Way Too Fast to Worry about Cholesterol
- I Live My Life a Quarter Mile at a Time
- I Think I'm Ready for the Pro Circuit!
- I'd Rather Ride Around with You
- If You Can't Run with the Big Dogs, Stay on the Porch
- It's the Journey, Not the Destination
- Ladies and Gentlemen, Start Your Engines!
- The Last Lap
- Life in the Fast Lane
- Life in the Slow Lane
- Life-Time Race Fan
- Life's Short—Drive Fast
- The Long and Winding Road
- Loop the Loop
- A Need for Speed
- Not So Fast
- The Older I Get, the Faster I Was
- On the Fast Track
- On the Other Side of Fear There is Freedom!
- On the Road Again
- On the Road Again... and Again... and Again
- On Track
- On Your Mark, Get Set, Go!
- One Lap to Go!
- Ooh! That Had to Hurt!
- Outpaced
- Pace Car
- Pit Crew
- Pit Stop
- Portrait of a Winner
- Put the Pedal to the Metal
- Qualifying
- Race Against the Clock
- A Race Can be Won or Lost in the Pits
- Race Car Drivers Love the Fast Lane

- The Race is On
- Race to the Finish
- Ready for the Pro-Circuit
- Real Cars are Made, Not Bought
- A Red Flag Warning
- Rev up the Engine
- Road Adventures USA
- Road Hog
- 'Round and 'Round
- Spin-Out
- Spin-Out at the Corner
- Sportsman-like Conduct
- Still Playing with Cars, after All These Years!
- Superstar
- Survival of the Fittest
- Tailgating
- Take It to the Limit
- Taking the Checkered Flag
- Taste of Victory
- There's No Looking Back Now
- They're Kissing Bumpers
- The Thrill of Victory
- Thrill Ride
- To Finish First, First You Have to Finish
- Today's Heroes

- Tools of the Trade
- Top Speed
- A Track Record
- Uneasy Rider
- Unrivaled
- Unrivaled Competition
- Victory Lap
- The Wheels on My Car Go 'Round and 'Round
- When the Week Ends, the Fun Begins
- Where the Blacktop Ends
- Where the Rubber Meets the Road
- White Flag—One Lap to Go!
- White Knuckles
- Winning with Style
- Your Mileage May Vary
- Zoom! Zoom! Zoom!
- Finishing races is important, but racing is more important. ~ Dale Earnhardt
- Aerodynamics are for people who cannot build engines. ~ Enzo Ferrari
- Auto racing, bull fighting and mountain climbing are the only real sports... all the others are games.
  ~ Ernest Hemmingway

- Horsepower has this tendency to break things. If you're not breaking anything, you're not going fast enough.

- Calling upon my years of experience, I froze at the controls. ~ Stirling Moss

- All I had to do is keep turning left! ~ George Robson

- I always ask God for blessings of protection on that person in the car, for blessings of protection on the crew as they're attending to the car on pit road. and I always ask for peace of mind for the wife.
  ~ Dale Beaver

- Faster, faster, faster until the thrill of speed overcomes the fear of death.
  ~ Hunter Thompson

- I feel safe when I'm on the racetrack, I really do. I know that I'm surrounded by the best drivers in the world. That's something you can't say when you're driving down the interstate. ~ Sterling Marlin

- I feel safer on a racetrack than I do on Houston's freeways. ~ A. J. Foyt

- I was doing fine till mid-corner, when I ran out of talent.

- If everything seems under control, you're just not going fast enough. ~ Mario Andretti

- If you're going to lead, then lead. If you're going to follow, get the hell out of my way!

- Anyone can drive a fast car, few can drive a car fast.

- I'm in the need—the need for speed! ~ Top Gun

- Never drive faster than your guardian angel can fly.

- I don't know driving in another way which isn't risky. Each one has to improve himself. Each driver has its limit. My limit is a little bit further than other's. ~ Ayrton Senna

- In the old days, drivers were fat and tires were skinny.

- It is amazing how many drivers, even at the Formula One level, think that the brakes are for slowing the car down.
  ~ Mario Andretti

- It is not always possible to be the best, but it is always possible to improve your own performance. ~ Jackie Stewart

- It's basically the same, just darker.
  ~ Alan Kulwicki

- Life may begin at 30, but it doesn't get real interesting until about 150.

- My biggest concern during a race is getting bored. The biggest thing I have to combat is falling asleep while going around and around. ~ Mario Andretti

- Never run out of real estate, traction, and ideas at the same time.

- The number of laps remaining is always one more than the amount of fuel left in the car.

- Once you've raced, you never forget it... and you never get over it. ~ Richard Childress

- The price for men in motion is the occasional collision. ~ Carroll Smith

- Oversteer is when your rear hits the wall. Understeer is when your face hits the wall!

- Oversteer scares passengers. Understeer scares drivers.

- Race cars are neither beautiful nor ugly. They become beautiful when they win. ~ Enzo Ferrari

- The crashes, people remember, but drivers remember the near misses. ~ Mario Andretti

- Racing is living; everything else is just waiting.

- Second place is the first loser. ~ Dennis Anderson

- Racing is the process of turning money into noise.

- Racing's less of a sport these days than commercial break doing 150 mph. ~ Peter Dunne

- Straights are for fast cars. Turns are for fast drivers.

- The cost of racing hasn't increased in 30 years. Back then, it took everything you had, and it still does.

- The number of times you get hit in a pileup is directly proportional to the number of times you said "I think it will go okay today."

- The shortest way between two points is a straight line. What's the fun in that?

- There's no secret. You just press the accelerator to the floor and steer left. ~ Bill Vukovich

- A part never breaks during a test session, only during a race.

- To achieve anything in this game you must be prepared to dabble in the boundary of disaster. ~ Sterling Moss

- What sets these—and all—racers apart from less daredevilish mortals is their complete lack of fear and their joy of doing something on the edge. They love to speed because it is dangerous.
  ~ Peter Golenback

- I'm not here to prove anything about being a woman. I'm here to drive a race car and try to win a race. ~ Lyn St. James

- That just shows you how important the car is in Formula One racing.
  ~ Murray Walker

- What's behind you doesn't matter. ~ Enzo Ferrai

- It'd be fun if we could run farther apart, but that's not going to sell many tickets. ~ Dale Earnhardt Jr.

- I'm just going to keep driving and have a good time doing it.
  ~ Dale Earnhardt Jr.

- When you win a race, you're on top that day, so take it for what its worth, have a good time and party 'cause the next day when you get out of bed, the meter goes back to zero again. ~ Bobby Allison

- Wrecks are going to happen in this business, that's just a risk of the sport. If you can't keep from worrying about it, then you're in the wrong line of work. ~ Coo Coo Marlin

- You win some, you lose some, you wreck some. ~ Dale Earnhardt

- If NASCAR racing gets any more exciting, I may not be able to stand it.
  ~ Roger Staubach

- When I look fast, I'm not smooth and I am going slowly. And when I look slow, I am smooth and going fast. ~Alain Prost

- You will never know the feeling of a driver when winning a race. The helmet hides feelings that cannot be understood. ~ Ayrton Senna

Badminton

- Are You Being Served?

- Badminton Baddie

- Badminton Battle!

- Badminton is for the Birdies

- Doubles Troubles

- Shuttle to the Moon

- Smash It!

- Swoosh!

- Watch the Birdie!
- What a Racquet!
- After picking up the racquet, I more than once wondered how far this could go. ~ Tony Gunawan
- It wouldn't be called badminton if we were good at it, right? ~ Bill Amend
- When badminton was accepted into the Barcelona Olympic Games it showed that there was an acceptance of my sport internationally.
  ~ Rhonda Cator

Band & Music

- All That Jazz
- Band is Not an Option—It's the Only Thing
- Band of Brothers/Sisters
- Band on the Run
- **Bee Bop** [bee embellishments]
- A Boomin' Band
- Can't You Hear the Music?
- Certified Band Geek (and Proud of It)
- Clef-Hangers
- Diva
- Do-Re-Me

- Earobics
- Familiar Refrain
- For the Love of Music
- The Gift of Music
- The Gift of Song
- Good Vibrations
- High Fidelity
- High Notes
- Homemade Music
- I Love a Parade
- If You Can't Play It Good, Play It Loud
- I'm Just a Singer in a Rock and Roll Band
- In My Heart There Rings a Melody
- It's Still Rock 'n' Roll to Me
- I've Got Rhythm
- Jazz It Up
- Jazzing
- Just a Note
- Kazoo Band
- Kazoos on Parade
- Keep on Singing
- Love is Just Friendship Set to Music
- Magical Musicians
- Make Your Own Kind of Music

- Moosicians Outstanding in Their Field
- Music from the Heart
- Music Has Charms to Soothe the Savage Beast
- Music is the Voice of the Angels
- The Music Man
- Music Notes
- Music of the Heart
- Music Soothes the Soul
- Music Teachers are Really #
- Music Teachers Hit the Right Note
- Musicians Duet Better!
- My Budding Musicians
- Note This
- Note-able
- On a Different Note
- One Man/Kid Band
- Outstanding Orchestra
- Perfect Harmony
- The Piano Man
- Playing by Ear
- Practice Makes Perfect
- Remember the Music
- Rock Around the Clock
- Rock 'n' Roll

- Say It with Music
- Sensational Symphony
- Sing, Sing a Song
- Singin' in the Rain
- Singin' Love's Tune
- Singin' the Blues
- Something to Sing About!
- The Sound of Music
- Sounds of Music
- Strike It Up
- Strike Up the Band
- Striking the Right Note
- Support the Arts—Kiss a Musician!
- There's Music in the Air
- Unchained Melody
- Up Tempo
- What a Glorious Noise
- An intellectual is someone who can listen to the William Tell Overture without thinking of the Lone Ranger. ~ John Chesson
- The harmony between friends is sweeter than any choir.
- A jazz musician is a juggler who uses harmonies instead of oranges. ~ Benny Green

A painter paints pictures on canvas, but musicians paint their pictures on silence. ~ Leopold Stokowski

• A song has a few rights, the same as ordinary citizens. If it happens to feel like flying where humans cannot fly—to scale mountains that are not there—who shall stop it? ~ Charles Ives

• After silence, that which comes nearest to expressing the inexpressible is music. ~ Aldous Huxley

• Alas for those that never sing, but die with all their music in them! ~ Oliver Wendell Holmes

• All deep things are song. It seems somehow the very central essence of us, song; as if all the rest were but wrappages and hulls! ~ Thomas Carlyle

• Classical music is the kind we keep thinking will turn into a tune. ~ Frank Mckinney

• Country music is three chords and the truth. ~ Harlan Howard

• He who hears music, feels his solitude peopled at once. ~ Robert Browning

• • He who sings scares away his woes. ~ Cervantes

• An artist, in giving a concert, should not demand an entrance fee but should ask the public to pay, just before leaving as much as they like. From the sum he would be able to judge what the world thinks of him—and we would have fewer mediocre concerts. ~ Kit Coleman

• Challenges make you discover things about yourself that you never really knew. They're what make the instrument stretch—what makes you go beyond the norm. ~ Cicely Tyson

• And the night shall be filled with music, and the cares that infest the day shall fold their tents like the Arabs and as silently steal away. ~ Longfellow

• Are we not formed, as notes of music are—for one another, though dissimilar? ~ Percy Bysshe Shelley

• I have my own particular sorrows, loves, delights; and you have yours. But sorrow, gladness, yearning, hope, love, belong to all of us, in all times and in all places. Music is the only means whereby we feel these emotions in their universality. ~ H.A. Overstreet

- Music is the poetry of the air. ~ Richter

- I think sometimes, could I only have music on my own terms; could I live in a great city, and know where I could go whenever I wished the ablution and inundation of musical waves,—that were a bath and a medicine.
  ~ Ralph Waldo Emerson

- Music is the wine that fills the cup of silence. ~ Robert Fripp

- Life can't be all bad when for ten dollars you can buy all the Beethoven sonatas and listen to them for ten years. ~ William F. Buckley, Jr.

- Music can noble hints impart, engender fury, kindle love, with unsuspected eloquence can move and manage all the man with secret art. ~ Joseph Addison

- When people hear good music, it makes them homesick for something they never had and never will have. ~ Edgar Watson Howe

- Music fills the infinite between two souls.
  ~ Rabindranath Tagore

- I worry that the person who thought up Muzak may be thinking up something else. ~ Lily Tomlin

- Music and rhythm find their way into the secret places of the soul. ~ Plato

- Music expresses that which cannot be said and on which it is impossible to be silent. ~ Victor Hugo

- If a composer could say what he had to say in words, he would not bother trying to say it in music. ~ Gustav Mahler

- Music is moonlight in the gloomy night of life.
  ~ Jean Paul Richter

- If I ever die of a heart attack, I hope it will be from playing my stereo too loud. ~ Unknown

- Music is the art which is most nigh to tears and memory. ~ Oscar Wilde

- If the king loves music, it is well with the land. ~ Mencius

- Music cleanses the understanding, inspires it and lifts it into a realm which it would not reach if it were left to itself.
  ~ Henry Ward Beecher

- In music the passions enjoy themselves. ~ Nietzsche

- Music has been my playmate, my lover and my crying towel.
  ~ Buffy Sainte-Marie

23

- It is incontestable that music induces in us a sense of the infinite and the contemplation of the invisible. ~ Victor De Laprade

- Its language is a language which the soul alone understands, but which the soul can never translate. ~ Arnold Bennett

- Make a joyful noise unto the Lord. ~ Psalms 98:4

- Men profess to be lovers of music, but for the most part they give no evidence in their opinions and lives that they have heard it. ~ Thoreau

- Most people use music as a couch; they want to be pillowed on it, relaxed and consoled for the stress of daily living. But serious music was never meant to be soporific. ~ Aaron Copland

- Music expresses feeling and thought, without language; it was below and before speech, and it is above and beyond all words. ~ Robert G. Ingersoll

- Music is a friend of labor for it lightens the task by refreshing the nerves and spirit of the worker. ~ William Green

- Bach opens a vista to the universe. After experiencing him, people feel there is meaning to life after all. ~ Helmut Walcha

- If anyone has conducted a Beethoven performance, and then doesn't have to go to an osteopath, then there's something wrong. ~ Simon Rattle

- If I were to begin life again, I would devote it to music. It is the only cheap and unpunished rapture upon earth. ~ Sydney Smith

- Music is an outburst of the soul. ~ Frederick Delius

- Music is love in search of a word. ~ Sidney Lanier

- Music is the literature of the heart; it commences where speech ends. ~ Alphonse De Lamartine

- Music is the mediator between the spiritual and the sensual life. ~ Beethoven

- Music is the medicine of the breaking heart. ~ Leigh Hunt

- Music is the shorthand of emotion. ~ Leo Tolstoy

- Music is the universal language of mankind. ~ Longfellow

- Music is the wine which inspires one to new generative processes, and I am Bacchus who presses out this glorious wine for mankind and makes them spiritually drunken.
  ~ Beethoven

- Silence is the fabric upon which the notes are woven. ~ Lawrence Duncan

- Music is well said to be the speech of angels.
  ~ Thomas Carlyle

- The joy of music should never be interrupted by a commercial.
  ~ Leonard Bernstein

- My whole trick is to keep the tune well out in front. If I play Tchaikovsky, I play his melodies and skip his spiritual struggle. ~ Liberace

- Take a music bath once or twice a week for a few seasons. You will find it is to the soul what a water bath is to the body.
  ~ Oliver Wendell Holmes

- The pause is as important as the note. ~ Truman Fisher

- Music is your own experience, your thoughts, your wisdom. If you don't live it, it won't come out of your horn. ~ Charlie Parker

- Music produces a kind of pleasure which human nature cannot do without.
  ~ Confucius

- The city is built to music, therefore never built at all, and therefore built forever.
  ~ Alfred Lord Tennyson

- Music rots when it gets too far from the dance. Poetry atrophies when it gets too far from music.
  ~ Ezra Pound

- Play the music, not the instrument. ~ Unknown

- Music that gentlier on the spirit lies, than tired eyelids upon tired eyes...
  ~ Alfred Lord Tennyson

- Opera is where a guy gets stabbed in the back, and instead of dying, he sings.
  ~ Robert Benchley

- The pleasure we obtain from music comes from counting, but counting unconsciously. Music is nothing but unconscious arithmetic.
  ~ Gottfried Wilhelm Leibniz

- Seventy-six trombones led the big parade. ~ Music Man

- Music was my refuge. I could crawl into the space between the notes and curl my back to loneliness.
  ~ Maya Angelou

- Music washes away from the soul the dust of everyday life. ~ Berthold Auerbach

- Music, once admitted to the soul, becomes a sort of spirit, and never dies. ~ Edward George Bulwer-Lytton

- Music, when soft voices die, vibrates in the memory. ~ Percy Bysshe Shelley

- Rock music in its lyrics often talks ahead of the time about what's going on in the country. ~ Edmund G. Brown

- There is no truer truth obtainable by man than comes of music. ~ Robert Browning

- My idea is that there is music in the air, music all around us; the world is full of it, and you simply take as much as you require. ~ Edward Elgar

- The discovery of song and the creation of musical instruments both owed their origin to a human impulse which lies much deeper than conscious intention: the need for rhythm in life... the need is a deep one, transcending thought and disregarded at our peril. ~ Richard Baker

- Music is what feelings sound like. ~ Unknown

- Music's the medicine of the mind. ~ John A. Logan

- Musical compositions, it should be remembered, do not inhabit certain countries, certain museums—like paintings and statues. The Mozart quintet is not shut up in Salzburg: I have it in my pocket. ~ Henri Rabaud

- The Irish gave the bagpipes to the Scots as a joke, but the Scots haven't got the joke yet. ~ Oliver Herford

- There is in souls a symphony with sounds: and as the mind is pitch'd the ear is pleased with melting airs, or martial, brisk or grave; some chord in unison with what we hear is touch'd within us, and the heart replies. ~ William Cowper

- There is nothing in the world so much like prayer as music is. ~ William P. Merrill

- • There's music in the sighing of a reed; there's music in the gushing of a rill; there's music in all things, if men had ears: their earth is but an echo of the spheres. ~ Lord Byron

26

- You are the music while the music lasts. ~ T.S. Eliot
- Without music life would be a mistake. ~ Nietzsche
- Were it not for music, we might in these days say, the beautiful is dead.
  ~ Benjamin Disraeli
- What passion cannot music raise and quell! ~ John Dryden
- The notes I handle no better than many pianists. But the pauses between the notes—ah, that is where the art resides!
  ~ Artur Schnabel
- What we provide is an atmosphere... of orchestrated pulse which works on people in a subliminal way. Under its influence I've seen shy debs and severe dowagers kick off their shoes and raise some wholesome hell. ~ Meyer Davis
- When words leave off, music begins. ~ Heinrich Heine
- Why waste money on psychotherapy when you can listen to the B Minor Mass? ~ Michael Torke
- You can't possibly hear the last movement of Beethoven's Seventh and go slow. ~ Oscar Levant

Baseball

- A Grand Slam
- And Listen to Those Cheers from the Crowd!
- Angels in the Outfield
- A Perfect Game
- Backyard Baseball
- Baseball Diamonds are a Boy's Best Friend
- Baseball: It's America's Pastime
- Baseball—It's Not Just a Game
- Bat Boy
- Batter Up!
- Better at the Ballpark
- Beware Curve Ball
- Casey at the Bat
- Catch Some Fun
- Conference on the Mound
- Diamond in the Rough
- Double Play
- Field of Dreams
- Fly Ball
- Foul Ball
- Game Day
- Going, Going, Gone!
- Grand Slam

- Havin' a Ball
- Hey-Batter-Batter
- Hit and Run
- Homerun!
- In a League All Your Own
- Life Lessons Learned in Little League
- Lil' Slugger
- Little Big League
- Little League, Big Dreams
- Major League Fun
- Minor League Fun
- MVP
- My Angel in the Outfield
- My Favorite Season? Baseball Season, Of Course!
- Never Argue with a .400 Hitter
- Nobody Loves the Ump
- On the Bench—Picking Up Slivers
- Pitcher Perfect
- Pitchin' In
- Play Ball
- Right Off the Bat
- Rookie of the Year
- Root, Root, Root for the Home Team
- Seventh Inning Stretch
- Sliiiiding into Home
- Slugger
- Stealing Second
- Steeeerike!
- Step up to the Plate
- Strike It Up
- Take State
- The Boys are Back in Town
- The Last Hit
- The Ol' Ball Game, Just New Players
- The Rookie
- Three Strikes, You're Out
- Triple Play
- We Want a Pitcher, Not a Belly-Itcher
- When My Son Pitches, They All Look like Strikes to Me
- World Series, Here We Come
- You'rrrrre Out!
- You'rrrrre Safe!
- I don't want them to forget Ruth; I just want them to remember me.
  ~ Hank Aaron
- I hate all hitters. I start a game mad and I stay that way until it's over.
  ~ Don Drysdale

- I swing big, with everything I've got. I hit big or I miss big. I like to live as big as I can. ~ Babe Ruth

- I would be lost without baseball. I don't think that I could stand being away from it as long as I was alive. ~ Roberto Clemente

- In the great department store of life, baseball is the toy department. ~ Unknown

- The American boy starts swinging the bat about as soon as he can lift one. ~ Tris Speaker

- The game's isn't over until it's over. ~ Yogi Berra

- The true harbinger of spring is not crocuses or swallows returning to Capistrano, but the sound of the bat on the ball. ~ Bill Veeck

- A knuckleball is a curve ball that doesn't give a damn. ~ Jimmy Cannon

- Like those special afternoons in summer when you go to Yankee Stadium at two o'clock in the afternoon for an eight o'clock game. It's so big, so empty and so silent that you can almost hear the sounds that aren't there. ~ Ray Miller

- A ball player's got to be kept hungry to become a big-leaguer. That's why no boy from a rich family ever made the big leagues. ~ Joe Dimaggio

- A baseball game is twice as much fun if you're seeing it on the company's time. ~ William C. Feather

- Baseball fans are junkies, and their heroin is the statistic. ~ Robert S. Wieder

- A game of great charm in the adoption of mathematical measurements to the timing of human movements, the exactitudes and adjustments of physical ability to hazardous chance. The speed of the legs, the dexterity of the body, the grace of the swing, the elusiveness of the slide—these are the features that make Americans everywhere forget the last syllable of a man's last name or the pigmentation of his skin. ~ Branch Rickey

- A baseball fan has the digestive apparatus of a billy goat. He can, and does, devour any set of diamond statistics with insatiable appetite and then nuzzles hungrily for more. ~ Arthur Daley

- A baseball park is the one place where a man's wife doesn't mind his getting excited over somebody else's curves. ~ Brendan Francis

- You can't hit what you can't see. ~ Walter Johnson

- A mystique of history and heritage surrounds the New York Yankees. It's like the old days revived. We're loved and hated, but always in larger doses than any other team. We're the only team in any sport whose name and uniform and insignia are synonymous with their entire sport all over the world. The Yankees mean baseball to more people than all the other teams combined. ~Paul Blair

- All requests for leave of absence on account of grandmother's funeral, sore throat, housecleaning, lame back, turning of the ringer, headaches, brain storm, cousin's wedding, general ailments or other legitimate excuses must be made out and handed to the boss not later than 10 a.m. on the morning of the game.
  ~ Traditional gag notice from a time when all games were played during daylight hours.

- All the fat guys watch me and say to their wives, "See, there's a fat guy doing okay. Bring me another beer." ~ Mickey Lolich

- Baseball happens to be a game of cumulative tension; but football, basketball and hockey are played with hand grenades and machine guns.
  ~ John Leonard

- A critic once characterized baseball as six minutes of action crammed into two-and-one-half hours.
  ~ Ray Fitzgerald

- Back then, my idol was Bugs Bunny, because I saw a cartoon of him playing ball— you know, the one where he plays every position himself with nobody else on the field but him? Now that I think of it, Bugs is still my idol. You have to love a ballplayer like that. ~ Nomar Garciaparra

- A hot dog at the ballgame beats roast beef at the Ritz. ~ Humphrey Bogart

- Baseball fans love numbers. They love to swirl them around their mouths like Bordeaux wine. ~ Pat Conroy

- Baseball has the great advantage over cricket of being sooner ended.
  ~ George Bernard Shaw

30

- Most ball games are lost, not won. ~ Casey Stengel

- Baseball is a ballet without music. Drama without words. ~ Ernie Harwell

- Say this much for big league baseball—it is beyond question the greatest conversation piece ever invented in America. ~ Bruce Catton

- Baseball is a game dominated by vital ghosts; it's a fraternity, like no other we have of the active and the no longer so, the living and the dead.
  ~ Richard Gilman

- Don't tell me about the world. Not today. It's springtime and they're knocking baseball around fields where the grass is damp and green in the morning and the kids are trying to hit the curve ball.
  ~ Pete Hamill

- Baseball is a harbor, a seclusion from failure that really matters, a playful utopia in which virtuosity can be savored to the third decimal place of a batting average. ~ Mark Kramer

- Baseball is an island of activity amidst a sea of statistics. ~ Unknown

- Baseball is almost the only orderly thing in a very unorderly world. If you get three strikes, even the best lawyer in the world can't get you off.
  ~ Bill Veeck

- Baseball is an allegorical play about America, a poetic, complex and subtle play of courage, fear, good luck, mistakes, patience about fate and sober self-esteem. ~ Saul Steinberg

- Baseball is drama with an endless run and an ever-changing cast. ~ Joe Garagiola

- I would like people not to think in terms of the 755 home runs I hit, but think in terms of what I've accomplished off the field and some of the things I stood for. ~ Hank Aaron

- Baseball is like a poker game. Nobody wants to quit when he's losing; nobody wants you to quit when you're ahead. ~ Jackie Robinson

- Every hitter likes fastballs, just like everybody likes ice cream. But you don't like it when someone's stuffing it into you by the gallon. That's what it feels like when Nolan Ryan's thrown balls by you. ~ Reggie Jackson

- Just give me 25 guys on the last year of their contracts; I'll win a pennant every year. ~ Sparky Anderso

- Baseball is made up of very few big and dramatic moments, but rather it's a beautifully put together pattern of countless little subtleties that finally add up to the big moment, and you have to be well-versed in the game to truly appreciate them. ~ Paul Richards

- Baseball is not necessarily an obsessive-compulsive disorder, like washing your hands 100 times a day, but it's beginning to seem that way. We're reaching the point where you can be a truly dedicated, state-of-the-art fan or you can have a life. Take your pick. ~ Thomas Boswell

- I see great things in baseball. It's our game—the American game. It will take our people out-of-doors, fill them with oxygen, give them a larger physical stoicism. ~ Walt Whitman

- Baseball is reassuring. It makes me feel as if the world is not going to blow up. ~ Sharon Olds

- Baseball is the only field of endeavor where a man can succeed three times out of ten and be considered a good performer. ~ Ted Williams

- England and America should scrap cricket and baseball and come up with a new game that they both can play. Like baseball, for example. ~ Robert Benchley

- Baseball is the only game left for people. To play basketball, you have to be 7 feet 6 inches. To play football, you have to be the same width. ~ Bill Veeck

- Baseball is the only sport I know that when you're on offense, the other team controls the ball. ~ Ken Harrelson

- Baseball is very big with my people. It figures. It's the only way we can get to shake a bat at a white man without starting a riot. ~ Dick Gregory

- Baseball is where boys practice being boys and men practice being boys, and they get real good at it. ~ Mary Cecile Leary

- Baseball isn't a business; it's more like a disease. ~ Walter F. O'Malley

- Baseball is the only major sport that appears backwards in a mirror.
  ~ George Carlin

- Baseball players are smarter than football players. How often do you see a baseball team penalized for too many men on the field? ~ Jim Bouton

- Love is the most important thing in the world, but baseball is pretty good too.
  ~ Greg, age 8

- Baseball, almost alone among our sports, traffics unashamedly and gloriously in nostalgia. For only baseball understands time and treats it with respect. The history of other sports seems to begin anew with each generation, but baseball, that wondrous myth of twentieth century America, gets passed on like an inheritance. ~ Stanley Cohen

- I have observed that baseball is not unlike war, and when you get right down to it, we batters are the heavy artillery. ~ Ty Cobb

- Poets are like baseball pitchers. Both have their moments. The intervals are the tough things.
  ~ Robert Frost

- Some people are born on third base and go through life thinking they hit a triple. ~ Barry Switzer

- Baseball statistics are like a girl in a bikini. They show a lot, but not everything.
  ~ Toby Harrah

- Baseball, to me, is still the national pastime because it is a summer game. I feel that almost all Americans are summer people, that summer is what they think of when they think of their childhood. I think it stirs up an incredible emotion within people.
  ~ Steve Busby

- Baseball, it is said, is only a game—true. And the Grand Canyon is only a hole in Arizona. ~ George F. Will

- Baseball brings to mind memories of the good old days when families gathered together for hot dogs, watermelon, soda pop and fun. It was a time when life was simpler, people had more time for family and fun. Children got their roots from just being together with relatives young and old. Baseball symbolized the goodness of life.

- Baseball? It's just a game—as simple as a ball and a bat. Yet, as complex as the American spirit it symbolizes. It's a sport, business, and sometimes even, religion. ~ Ernie Harwell,

- Character, courage, loyalty. ~ Little League Motto

- I have discovered in twenty years of moving around a ballpark, that the knowledge of the game is usually in inverse proportion to the price of the seats. ~ Bill Veeck

- I didn't get over 1300 walks without knowing the strike zone. ~ Wade Boggs

- Basketball, hockey and track meets are action heaped upon action, climax upon climax, until the onlooker's responses become deadened. Baseball is for the leisurely afternoons of summer and for the unchanging dreams. ~ Roger Kahn

- I ain't ever had a job. I just always played baseball.
  ~ Leroy 'Satchel' Paige

- Being with a woman all night never hurt no professional baseball player. It's staying up all night looking for a woman that does him in.
  ~ Casey Stengel

- Buy me some peanuts and Cracker Jack—I don't care if I ever get back!
  ~ Jack Norworth

- Don't forget to swing hard, in case you hit the ball. ~ Woodie Held

- Don't look back. Something may be gaining on you.
  ~ Satchel Paige

- Baseball is almost the only place in life where a sacrifice is really appreciated. ~ Mark Beltaire

- Baseball is too much of a sport to be called a business and too much of a business to be called a sport. ~ Philip Wrigley

- Every player should be accorded the privilege of at least one season with the Chicago Cubs. That's baseball as it should be played—in God's own sunshine. And that's really living. ~ Alvin Dark

- Every strike brings me closer to the next home run. ~ Babe Ruth

- First triple I ever had.
  ~ Lefty Gomez, on his heart bypass surgery

- For it's one, two, three strikes you're out at the old ball game! ~ Jack Norworth

- For the parent of a little leaguer, a baseball game is simply a nervous breakdown divided into innings. ~ Earl Wilson

- Gibson pitches as though he's double-parked.
  ~ Vin Scully, on Bob Gibson

- Good pitching will beat good hitting any time—and vice versa. ~ Bob Veale

- The crowd makes the ballgame. ~ Ty Cobb

- It's no coincidence that female interest in the sport of baseball has increased greatly since the ballplayers swapped those wonderful old-time baggy flannel uniforms for leotards. ~ Mike Royko

- Hating the New York Yankees is as American as apple pie, unwed mothers and cheating on your income tax. ~ Mike Royko

- He's got power enough to hit home runs in any park, including Yellowstone.
  ~ Sparky Anderson

- I don't care how long you've been around; you'll never see it all. ~ Bob Lemon

- Hitting is timing. Pitching is upsetting timing.
  ~ Warren Spahn

- I became a good pitcher when I stopped trying to make them miss the ball and started trying to make them hit it. ~ Sandy Koufax

- I believe in the church of baseball. I tried all the major religions and most of the minor ones. I've worshipped Buddha, Allah, Brahma, Vishnu, Siva, trees, mushrooms and Isadora Duncan. I know things. For instance, there are 108 beads in a Catholic rosary and there are 108 stitches in a baseball. When I learned that, I gave Jesus a chance.
  ~ Ron Shelton

- I didn't teach you that. Catch the ball with your glove.
  ~ Willie Mays, on his famous barehanded catch

- I don't love baseball. I don't love most of today's players. I don't love the owners. I do love, however, the baseball that is in the heads of baseball fans. I love the dreams of glory of 10-year-olds, the reminiscences of 70-year-olds. The greatest baseball arena is in our heads, what we bring to the games, to the telecasts, to reading newspaper reports.
  ~ Stan Isaacs

- I don't want to play golf. When I hit a ball, I want someone else to go chase it. ~ Rogers Hornsby

- I can't very well tell my batters don't hit it to him. Wherever they hit it, he's there anyway.
  ~ Gil Hodges, on Willie Mays

- He hit the ball so hard, I couldn't even turn around in time to see it go over the fence. ~ Roger Clemens

- I had a better year.
  ~ Babe Ruth, on why he was demanding a salary larger than President Hoover's

- I had all my own teeth and I wanted to keep it that way.
  ~ Tom Glavine, on why he played baseball, not hockey

- I keep my eyes clear and I hit 'em where they ain't.
  ~ Willie Keeler, explaining his .432 average

- I know a man who is a diamond cutter. He mows the lawn at Yankee Stadium. ~ Henny Youngman

- Baseball was made for kids, and grown-ups only screw it up. ~ Bob Lemon

- If God wanted football played in the spring, he would not have invented baseball. ~ Sam Rutigliano

- I was playing it like Willie Wilson, but I forgot that I'm in Clint Hurdle's body.
  ~ Clint Hurdle

- I was such a dangerous hitter I even got intentional walks in batting practice.
  ~ Casey Stengel

- Blind people come to the park just to hear him pitch. ~ Reggie Jackson

- If I had my career to play over, one thing I'd do differently is swing more. Those 1,200 walks I got, nobody remembers them.
  ~ Pee Wee Reese

- With those who don't give a damn about baseball, I can only sympathize. I do not resent them. I am even willing to concede that many of them are physically clean, good to their mothers and in favor of world peace. But while the game is on, I can't think of anything to say to them. ~ Art Hill

- If I were playing third base and my mother were rounding third with the run that was going to beat us, I'd trip her. Oh, I'd pick her up and brush her off and say, "Sorry, Mom," but nobody beats me. ~ Leo Durocher

- If a woman has to choose between catching a fly ball and saving an infant's life, she will choose to save the infant's life without even considering if there are men on base. ~ Dave Barry

- Life will always throw you curves, just keep fouling them off... The right pitch will come, but when it does, be prepared to run the bases. ~ Rick Maksian

- I'm convinced that every boy, in his heart, would rather steal second base than an automobile. ~ Tom Clark

- It breaks your heart. It is designed to break your heart. The game begins in spring, when everything else begins again, and it blossoms in the summer, filling the afternoons and evenings, and then as soon as the chill rains come, it stops and leaves you to face the fall alone.
  ~ A. Bartlett Giamatti

- It is well to remember that a Martian observing his first baseball game would be quite correct in concluding that the last two words of the national anthem are: PLAY BALL!
  ~ Herbert H. Paper

- Never win twenty games a year, because then they'll expect you to do it every year. ~ Pitcher Billy Loes

- More than any other American sport, baseball creates the magnetic, addictive illusion that it can almost be understood.
  ~ Thomas Boswell

- It actually giggles at you as it goes by.
  ~ Rick Monday, on Phil Niekro's knuckleball

- It never ceases to amaze me how many of baseball's wounds are self-inflicted.
  ~ Bill Veeck

- It's hard to win a pennant, but it's harder losing one.
  ~ Chuck Tanner

- It's not over till it's over.
  ~ Yogi Berra

- Baseball is a game where a curve is an optical illusion, a screwball can be a pitch or a person, stealing is legal and you can spit anywhere you like except in the umpire's eye or on the ball. ~ Jim Murray

- I've come to the conclusion that the two most important things in life are good friends and a good bullpen. ~ Bob Lemon

- Ninety feet between home plate and first base may be the closest man has ever come to perfection. ~ Red Smith

- No game in the world is as tidy and dramatically neat as baseball, with cause and effect, crime and punishment, motive and result, so cleanly defined. ~ Paul Gallico

- It's an announced test, so you not only failed the steroid test, you failed the IQ test.
  ~ Bob Costas, on players who test positive for steroids

- Leo Durocher is a man with an infinite capacity for making a bad thing worse.
  ~ Branch Rickey, on his manager

- If it weren't for baseball, many kids wouldn't know what a millionaire looked like. ~ Phyllis Diller

- More than any other games, baseball gives its players space—both physical and emotional—in which to define themselves. ~ John Eskow

- If a horse can't eat it, I don't want to play on it.
  ~ Dick Allen, on artificial turf

- It ain't like football. You can't make up no trick plays. ~ Yogi Berra

- My motto was to keep swinging. Whether I was in a slump or feeling badly or having trouble off the field, the only thing to do was to keep swinging. ~ Hank Aaron

- No matter how good you are, you're going to lose one-third of your games. No matter how bad you are you're going to win one-third of your games. It's the other third that makes the difference.
  ~ Tommy Lasorda

- Just take the ball and throw it where you want to. Throw strikes. Home plate don't move.
  ~ Leroy "Satchel" Paige

- Man, if I made a million dollars, I would come in at six in the morning, sweep the stands, wash the uniforms, clean out the offices, manage the team, and play the game.
  ~ Duke Snider, on salary disputes

- My dad taught me to switch-hit. He and my grandfather, who was left -handed, pitched to me everyday after school in the back yard. I batted lefty against my dad and righty against my granddad. ~ Mickey Mantle

- No one wants to hear about the labor pains, they just want to see the baby. ~ Lou Brock

- Rooting for the Yankees is like rooting for the house in black jack. ~ Adam Morrow

- Nolan Ryan is pitching much better now that he has his curve ball straightened out. ~ Joe Garagiola

- One of the chief duties of the fan is to engage in arguments with the man behind him. This department of the game has been allowed to run down fearfully. ~ Robert Benchley

- The designated hitter rule is like letting someone else take Wilt Chamberlain's free throws. ~ Rick Wise

- Baseball is a fun game. It beats working for a living. ~ Phil Linz

- Sandy's fastball was so fast, some batters would start to swing as he was on his way to the mound. ~ Jim Murray

- People ask me what I do in winter when there's no baseball. I'll tell you what I do. I stare out the window and wait for spring. ~ Rogers Hornsby

- Pitchers, like poets, are born not made. ~ Cy Young

- Progress always involves risks. You can't steal second base and keep your foot on first. ~ Frederick B. Wilcox

- Pro-rated at 500 at-bats a year; that means that for two years out of the fourteen I played, I never even touched the ball. ~ Norm Cash, on his 1,081 strikeouts

- Reading about baseball is a lot more interesting than reading about chess, but you have to wonder: don't any of these guys ever go fishing? ~ Dave Shiflett

- Spread the diaper in the position of the diamond with you at bat. Then fold second base down to home and set the baby on the pitcher's mound. Put first base and third together, bring up home plate and pin the three together. Of course, in case of rain, you gotta call the game and start all over again. ~ Jimmy Piersall

- Strikeouts are boring—besides that, they're fascist. Throw some ground balls. More democratic. ~ Ron Shelton

- During my 18 years I came to bat almost 10,000 times. I struck out about 1,700 times and walked maybe 1,800 times. You figure a ballplayer will average about 500 at-bats a season. That means I played seven years without ever hitting the ball. ~ Mickey Mantle

- The great thing about baseball is that there's a crisis every day. ~ Gabe Paul

- The great trouble with baseball today is that most of the players are in the game for the money and that's it, not for the love of it, the excitement of it, the thrill of it. ~ Ty Cobb

- The charm of baseball is that, dull as it may be on the field, it is endlessly fascinating as a rehash. ~ Jim Murray

- Take me out to the ball game. Take me out to the crowd. Buy me some peanuts and Cracker Jack. I don't care if I ever get back. We'll root, root, root for the home team. If they don't win, it's a shame. For it's one, two, three strikes, your out, at the old ball game. ~ Jack Norworth

- Slumps are like a soft bed. They're easy to get into and hard to get out of. ~ Johnny Bench

- What does a mama bear on the pill have in common with the World Series? No cubs. ~ Harry Caray

- The best way to catch a knuckleball is to wait until the ball stops rolling and then pick it up. ~ Bob Uecker

- When they start the game, they don't yell, "work ball." They say, "play ball." ~ Willie Stargell

- Well, boys, it's a round ball and a round bat and you got to hit the ball square. ~ Joe Schultz

- The only way to pitch to him is inside, so you force him to pull the ball. That way the line drive won't hit you. ~ Rudy May, on George Brett

- There are only two places in the league. First and no place. ~ Tom Seaver

- Putting lights in Wrigley Field is like putting aluminum siding on the Sistine Chapel. ~ Roger Simon

- You can learn little from victory. You can learn everything from defeat. ~ Christy Mathewson

- The greatest feeling in the world is to win a major league game. The second-greatest feeling is to lose a major league game.
  ~ Chuck Tanner

- Wives of ballplayers, when they teach their children their prayers, should instruct them how to say: "God bless mommy, God bless daddy, God bless Babe Ruth. Babe Ruth has upped daddy's paycheck by fifteen to forty percent."
  ~ Waite Hoyt

- The pitcher has got only a ball. I've got a bat. So the percentage of weapons is in my favor and I let the fellow with the ball do the fretting. ~ Hank Aaron

- The pitcher has to find out if the hitter is timid. And if the hitter is timid, he has to remind the hitter he's timid. ~ Don Drysdale

- You owe it to yourself to be the best you can possible be—in baseball and in life. ~ Pete Rose

- The place was always cold, and I got the feeling that the fans would have enjoyed baseball more if it had been played with a hockey puck. ~ Andre Dawson

- The other sports are just sports. Baseball is a love.
  ~ Bryant Gumbell

- Why does everybody stand up and sing "Take Me Out to the Ballgame" when they're already there?
  ~ Larry Anderson

- The season starts too early and finishes too late and there are too many games in between. ~ Bill Veeck

- You spend a good piece of your life gripping a baseball, and in the end it turns out that it was the other way around all the time. ~ Jim Bouton

- There have been only two geniuses in the world: Willie Mays and Willie Shakespeare.
  ~ Tallulah Bankhead

- There is always some kid who may be seeing me for the first or last time. I owe him my best. ~ Joe Dimaggio

- There's nothing wrong with the Little League World Series that locking out the adults couldn't cure.
  ~ Mike Penner

- The difference between this guy and the rest of us is that when we get hot we go up to .300. When he gets hot he goes up to .500.
  ~ Doug DeCinces, on Rod Carew

- That's baseball, and it's my game. Y' know, you take your worries to the game, and you leave 'em there. You yell like crazy for your guys. It's good for your lungs, gives you a lift and nobody calls the cops. Pretty girls, lots of 'em.
  ~ Humphrey Bogart

- When Steve and I die, we are going to be buried in the same cemetery, 60 feet, 6 inches apart.
  ~ Tim Mccarver, who caught all of Steve Carlton's games

- This is a game to be savored, not gulped. There's time to discuss everything between pitches or between innings. ~ Bill Veeck

- When we played softball, I'd steal second base, feel guilty and go back. ~ Woody Allen

- Baseball and cricket are beautiful and highly stylized medieval war substitutes, chess made flesh, a mixture of proud chivalry and base—in both senses—greed. ~ John Fowles

- Trying to sneak a pitch past Hank Aaron is like trying to sneak a sunrise past a rooster.
  ~ Attrib. to Joe Adcock and Curt Simmons

- Two-thirds of the earth is covered by water. The other one-third is covered by Gary Maddox.
  ~ Ralph Kiner, on the outfielder

- Things could be worse. Suppose your errors were counted and published every day, like those of a baseball player. ~ Unknown

- The strongest thing that baseball has going for it today are its yesterdays.
  ~ Lawrence Ritter

- This is nothing. I've got nine writers standing here. McGuire had 200 writers when he had 30 home runs.
  ~ Barry Bonds

- When you're in a slump, it's almost as if you look out at the field and it's one big glove. ~ Vance Law

- What is both surprising and delightful is that spectators are allowed, and even expected, to join in the vocal part of the game...There is no reason why the field should not try to put the batsman off his stroke at the critical moment by neatly timed disparagements of his wife's fidelity and his mother's respectability.
  ~ George Bernard Shaw

- Watching a spring training game is as exciting as watching a tree form its annual ring. ~ Jerry Izenberg

- The way a team plays as a whole determines its success. You may have the greatest bunch of individual stars in the world, but if they don't play together, the club won't be worth a dime. ~ Babe Ruth

- When you're ten, you know more about your team than you ever will know again. ~ Dan Shaughnessy

- With tears in my eyes. ~ Frank Sullivan, on how he pitched to Mickey Mantle

- You know you're pitching well when the batters look as bad as you do at the plate. ~ Duke Snider

- There are three things in my life which I really love: God, my family, and baseball. The only problem—once baseball season starts, I change the order around a bit. ~ Al Gallagher

- You gotta be a man to play baseball for a living, but you gotta have a lot of little boy in you, too. ~ Roy Campanella

- Slump? I ain't in no slump. I just ain't hitting. ~ Yogi Berra

- To a pitcher, a base hit is the perfect example of negative feedback. ~ Steve Hovley

- You don't save a pitcher for tomorrow. Tomorrow it may rain. ~ Leo Durocher

- Baseball is ninety percent mental, and the other half is physical. ~ Yogi Berra

- You know it's summertime at Candlestick when the fog rolls in, the wind kicks up and you see the center fielder slicing open a caribou to survive the ninth inning. ~ Bob Sarlette

- There are two theories on hitting the knuckleball. Unfortunately, neither of them work. ~ Charlie Lau

Basketball

- Air Ball!
- Alley-Oop to the Hoop
- Around the Rim
- Attitude is Everything!
- B-Ball
- Basketball Jones
- Basketball is Life, Nothing Else Matters!
- Basketball—Not Just a Game

- Basket Case
- Baskets of Fun
- Box Out!
- Build the Spirit
- Chairmen of the Boards
- Cinderella Goes to the Ball... and Takes It to the Net
- Court Side
- Crashin' the Boards
- Dishin' and Swishin'
- Dribble, Pass, Shoot
- Dribble, Rebound, Shoot, Score!
- Drivin' or Dishin'... Points or Assists !
- Final Four
- Full Court Press
- Go for the Three
- Hands up! Block That Shot!
- Hang Time
- Hit the Net!
- Hittin' the Shot
- Holdin' Court
- Hoop-Dee-Doo
- Hoop Dreams
- Hoop Heaven
- Hoop, There It is!
- Hoopin' It Up

- Hoopla
- Hoops Anyone?
- H-O-R-S-E
- Hot Shot
- I am Woman, See Me Score!
- In the Air Tonight
- In the Paint
- Intentional Foul
- It's an Easy Two!
- It's Not the Hype, It's the Hoop!
- Jam Session
- King/Queen of the Court
- Kiss the Rim
- Like Mike
- March Madness
- My Momma Taught Me That
- Nothing But Net
- On the Bench—Picking Up Slivers
- Open Shot
- Overtime
- Pass... Shoot... Score
- Play Ball
- Poppin' the Three!
- Pound the Boards
- Put It Through for Two

- Put Me in Coach!
- Rip It!
- Rip Off the Tip Off
- Shootin' Hoops
- Sink It and Win!
- Sink That Shot!
- Slam Dunk
- Slammin' and Jammin'
- Swwwwiiiish!
- Take It to the Hoop
- Taking It Home
- Take the Ball and Run with It
- The Hoopster
- The Rim Reapers
- Time Out
- To "Air" is Human
- Turning the Team Around 360 Degrees
- Walk This Way
- We've Got the Hoopla!
- Whoop It Up
- Whoosh!
- Work the Crowd
- Wow! That was a Slam Dunk!
- You Miss 100% of the Shots You Don't Take
- Zero Gravity

- A tough day at the office is even tougher when your office contains spectator seating. ~ Nik Posa
- Everybody pulls for David; nobody roots for Goliath. ~ Wilt Chamberlain
- Basketball is like photography, if you don't focus, all you have is the negative. ~ Dan Frisby
- Basketball is like war in that offensive weapons are developed first, and it always takes a while for the defense to catch up. ~ Red Auerbach
- Any American boy can be a basketball star if he grows up, up, up. ~ Bill Vaughn
- Be strong in body, clean in mind, lofty in ideals. ~ James Naismith, creator
- First master the fundamentals. ~ Larry Bird
- Boards, boards, boards. ~ Knute Rockne
- Giving "Magic" the basketball is like giving Hitler an army, Jesse James a gang, or Genghis Khan a horse. ~ Jim Murray
- Good, better, best. Never let it rest. Until your good is better and your better is best. ~ Tim Duncan

- I don't need glory, I don't need fame, I don't need the spotlight—I just need the ball! ~ Unknown

- I hate it. It looks like a stickup at 7-Eleven. Five guys standing there with their hands in the air. ~ Norm Sloan, on zone defense

- Basketball doesn't build character it reveals it. ~ Unknown

- I haven't been able to slam-dunk the basketball for the past five years. Or for the thirty-eight years before that, either. ~ Dave Barry

- I liked the choreography, but I didn't care for the costumes. ~ Tommy Tune, on why he never played basketball

- I've never had major knee surgery on any other part of my body. ~ Winston Bennett

- If all I'm remembered for is being a good basketball player, then I've done a bad job with the rest of my life. ~ Isiah Thomas

- I try to do the right thing at the right time. They may just be little things, but usually they make the difference between winning and losing. ~ Kareem Abdul-Jabbar

- If the NBA were on channel 5 and a bunch of frogs making love were on channel 4, I'd watch the frogs, even if they were coming in fuzzy. ~ Bobby Knight

- Basketball is the MTV of sports. ~ Sara Levinson

- If you are going to take it to the bank, then you better cash it in. ~ Shannon Fish

- Fans never fall asleep at our games because they're afraid they might get hit by a pass. ~ George Raveling

- If you meet the Buddha in the lane, feed him the ball. ~ Phil Jackson

- I've always believed that if you put in the work, the results will come... I don't do things half-heartedly. Because I know if I do, then I can expect half-hearted results. ~ Michael Jordon

- I've learned I can't help the team sitting on the bench. ~ Wilt Chamberlain

- Left hand, right hand, it doesn't matter. I'm amphibious. ~ Charles Shackleford

- We're shooting 100 percent—60 percent from the field and 40 percent from the free-throw line. ~ Norm Stewart

- My responsibility is getting all my players playing for the name on the front of the jersey, not the one on the back. ~ Unknown

- When it's played the way it's spozed to be played, basketball happens in the air; flying, floating, elevated above the floor, levitating the way oppressed peoples of this earth imagine themselves in their dreams.
  ~ John Edgar Wideman

- Nothing there but basketball, a game which won't be fit for people until they set the basket umbilicus-high and return the giraffes to the zoo.
  ~ Ogden Nash

- What you are as a person is far more important than what you are as a basketball player.
  ~ John Wooden

- Of course I can see better than the referee, I'm a parent!

- One man can be a crucial ingredient on a team, but one man cannot make a team. ~ Kareem Abdul-Jabbar

- Sometimes a player's greatest challenge is coming to grips with his role on the team. ~ Scottie Pippen

- The idea is not to block every shot. The idea is to make your opponent believe that you might block every shot. ~ Bill Russell

- The invention of basketball was not an accident. It was developed to meet a need. Those boys simply would not play "drop the handkerchief."
  ~ James Naismith

- The only difference between a good shot and a bad shot is if it goes in or not. ~ Charles Barkley

- I'm tired of hearing about money, money, money, money, money. I just want to play the game, drink Pepsi, wear Reebok.
  ~ Shaquille O'Neal

- The rule was "no autopsy, no foul."
  ~ Stewart Granger, on the pick-up games of his childhood

- You don't play against opponents. You play against the game of basketball. ~ Bobby Knight

- When I was young, I never wanted to leave the court until I got things exactly correct. My dream was to become a pro. ~ Larry Bird

- To win, you've got to put the ball in the macramé.
  ~ Terry Mcguire

47

- When I dunk, I put something on it. I want the ball to hit the floor before I do. ~ Darryl Dawkins

- These are my new shoes. They're good shoes. They won't make you rich like me, they won't make you rebound like me, they definitely won't make you handsome like me. They'll only make you have shoes like me. That's it.
  ~ Charles Barkley in a commercial

- They said playing basketball would kill me. Well, not playing basketball was killing me. ~ Magic Johnson

- We have a great bunch of outside shooters. Unfortunately, all our games are played indoors.
  ~ Weldon Drew

- This is the second most exciting indoor sport, and the other one shouldn't have spectators. ~ Dick Vertlieb

- There are really only two plays: Romeo and Juliet, and put the darn ball in the basket. ~ Abe Lemons

- What is so fascinating about sitting around watching a bunch of pituitary cases stuff a ball through a hoop?
  ~ Woody Allen

- They say that nobody is perfect. Then they tell you practice makes perfect. I wish they'd make up their minds. ~ Wilt Chamberlain

- When I went to Catholic high school in Philadelphia, we just had one coach for football and basketball. He took all of us who turned out and had us run through a forest. The ones who ran into the trees were on the football team. ~ George Raveling

- The secret is to have eight great players and four others who will cheer like crazy. ~ Jerry Tarkanian

- When you miss a shot, never think of what you did wrong. Take the next shot thinking of what you must do right. ~ Tony Alfonso

- There are two things in life: basketball and more basketball.

- What you are as a person is far more important than what you are as a basketball player. ~ John Wooden

- You can run a lot of plays when your X is twice as big as the other guys' O. It makes your X's and O's pretty good. ~ Paul Westphal

Bicycling

- All Terrain
- Bicycle Race
- The Big Wheel
- Biker Babe
- Born to Ride
- Breaking Away
- Cyclists Don't Reinvent the Wheel—They Reinvent Speed
- Cyclists Make the World Go Round
- Don't Yank My Chain!
- Easy Rider
- Get in Gear
- Handlebar Mustache
- Hell on Wheels
- Lean on the Curves
- Life Cyclist
- A Need for Speed
- Off the Beaten Trail
- Pedal Power
- Pedal to the Metal
- Pedal Pushers
- Put a Spoke in His/Her Wheel
- The Race is On
- Ride Like the Wind
- Set the Wheels in Motion
- Slow and Steady Wins the Race
- Spinning His/Her Wheels
- The Squeaky Wheel
- Switch Gears
- Third Wheel
- Un-Easy Rider
- A Vicious Cyclist
- The Wheel of Life
- Wheeler-Dealer
- The Wheels are Turning
- Wheel-y Wonderful
- Where the Rubber Meets the Road
- Bicycling is the nearest approximation I know to the flight of birds. The airplane simply carries a man on its back like an obedient Pegasus; it gives him no wings of his own.
  ~ Louis J. Helle, Jr.
- All creatures who have ever walked have wished that they might fly. With high wheelers, a flesh and blood man can hitch wings to his feet. ~ Karl Kron
- Think of bicycles as rideable art that can just about save the world.
  ~ Grant Petersen

- Cycle tracks will abound in utopia. ~ H.G. Wells

- The bicycle is the most efficient machine ever created: converting calories into gas, a bicycle gets the equivalent of three thousand miles per gallon. ~ Bill Strickland

- A bicycle does get you there and more... and there is always the thin edge of danger to keep you alert and comfortably apprehensive. Dogs become dogs again and snap at your raincoat; potholes become personal. And getting there is all the fun. ~ Bill Emerson

- Get a bicycle. You will not regret it if you live.
  ~ Mark Twain

- It is by riding a bicycle that you learn the contours of a country best, since you have to sweat up the hills and coast down them. Thus you remember them as they actually are, while in a motor car only a high hill impresses you, and you have no such accurate remembrance of country you have driven through as you gain by riding a bicycle.
  ~ Hemingway

- The bicycle will accomplish more for women's sensible dress than all the reform movements that have ever been waged. ~ Unknown

- All bicycles weigh fifty pounds. A thirty-pound bicycle needs a twenty-pound lock. A forty-pound bicycle needs a ten-pound lock. A fifty-pound bicycle doesn't need a lock.
  ~ Unknown

- Consider a man riding a bicycle. Whoever he is, we can say three things about him. We know he got on the bicycle and started to move. We know that at some point he will stop and get off. Most important of all, we know that if at any point between the beginning and the end of his journey he stops moving and does not get off the bicycle he will fall off it. That is a metaphor for the journey through life of any living thing, and I think of any society of living things. ~ William Golding

- It never gets easier, you just go faster. ~ Greg Lemond

- Kansas: home of the highway with 318 miles and 11 curves.

- Messengers and mountain bikers share a common chromosome. ~ James Bethea

- The bicycle is just as good company as most husbands and, when it gets old and shabby, a woman can dispose of it and get a new one without shocking the entire community. ~ Ann Strong

- Cycling is unique. No other sport lets you go like that—where there's only the bike left to hold you up. If you ran as hard, you'd fall over. Your legs wouldn't support you.
  ~ Steve Johnson

- First law of bicycling: No matter which way you ride, it's uphill and against the wind. ~ Gianna Bellofatto

- After your first day of cycling, one dream is inevitable. A memory of motion lingers in the muscles of your legs, and 'round and 'round they seem to go. You ride through dreamland on wonderful dream bicycles that change and grow.
  ~ H.G. Wells

- What do you call a cyclist who doesn't wear a helmet? An organ donor.
  ~ David Perry

- I took care of my wheel as one would look after a Rolls Royce. ~ Henry Miller

- Melancholy is incompatible with bicycling. ~ James E. Starrs

- If you ride, you know those moments when you have fed yourself into the traffic, felt the hashed-up asphalt rattle in the handlebars, held a lungful of air in a cloud of exhaust. Up ahead there are two parallel buses. With cat's whiskers, you measure the clearance down a doubtful alley. You swing wide, outflank that flower truck. The cross-street yellow light is turning red. You burst off the green like a surfer on a wave of metal. You have a hundred empty yards of Broadway to yourself.
  ~ Chip Brown

- Get me on that machine and I have to go. I go scorching along the road and cursing aloud at myself for doing it.
  ~ H.G. Wells

- Until mountain biking came along, the bike scene was ruled by a small elite cadre of people who seemed allergic to enthusiasm.
  ~ Jacquie Phelan

- Think of the hopes, the dreams, the effort, the brilliance, the pure force of will that, over the eons, has gone into the creation of the Cadillac Coupe De Ville. Bicycle riders would have us throw all this on the ash heap of history. ~ P.J. O'Rourke

- Why should anyone steal a watch when he could steal a bicycle? ~ Flann O'Brien

- The bicycle, the bicycle surely, should always be the vehicle of novelists and poets. ~ Christopher Morley

- It is curious that with the advent of the automobile and the airplane, the bicycle is still with us. Perhaps people like the world they can see from a bike or the air they breathe when they're out on a bike. Or they like the bicycle's simplicity and the precision with which it is made. Or because they like the feeling of being able to hurtle through air one minute and saunter through a park the next, without leaving behind clouds of choking exhaust, without leaving behind so much as a footstep. ~ Gurdon S. Leete

- The secret to mountain biking is pretty simple. The slower you go the more likely it is you'll crash. ~ Julie Furtado

- Pain is a big fat creature riding on your back. The farther you pedal, the heavier he feels. The harder you push, the tighter he squeezes your chest. The steeper the climb, the deeper he digs his jagged, sharp claws into your muscles. ~ Scott Martin

- Nothing compares to the simple pleasure of a bike ride. ~ John F. Kennedy

- Mankind has invested more than four million years of evolution in the attempt to avoid physical exertion. Now a group of backward-thinking atavists mounted on foot-powered pairs of hula-hoops would have us pumping our legs, gritting our teeth and searing our lungs as though we were being chased across the Pleistocene savanna by saber-toothed tigers. ~ P.J. O'Rourke

- You never have the wind with you—either it is against you or you're having a good day. ~ Daniel Behrman

52

- Tens of thousands who could never afford to own, feed and stable a horse, had by this bright invention enjoyed the swiftness of motion which is perhaps the most fascinating feature of material life. ~ Frances Willard

- The bicycle is a curious vehicle. Its passenger is its engine. ~ John Howard

- Most bicyclists in New York City obey instinct far more than they obey the traffic laws, which is to say that they run red lights, go the wrong way on one-way streets, violate cross-walks, and terrify innocents, because it just seems easier that way. Cycling in the city, and particularly in midtown, is anarchy without malice.
  ~ New Yorker

- The bicycle had—and still has—a humane, almost classical moderation in the kind of pleasure it offers. It is the kind of machine that a Hellenistic Greek might have invented and ridden. It does no violence to our normal reactions, it does not pretend to free us from our normal environment. ~ J.B. Jackson

- The hardest part of raising a child is teaching them to ride bicycles. A shaky child on a bicycle for the first time needs both support and freedom. The realization that this is what the child will always need can hit hard. ~ Sloan Wilson

- When I see an adult on a bicycle, I do not despair for the future of the human race. ~ H.G. Wells

- The bicycle is the most civilized conveyance known to man. Other forms of transport grow daily more nightmarish. Only the bicycle remains pure in heart. ~ Iris Murdoch

- When I go biking, I repeat a mantra of the day's sensations: bright sun, blue sky, warm breeze, blue jay's call, ice melting and so on. This helps me transcend the traffic, ignore the clamorings of work, leave all the mind theaters behind and focus on nature instead. I still must abide by the rules of the road, of biking, of gravity. But I am mentally far away from civilization. The world is breaking someone else's heart.
  ~Diane Ackerman

- It would not be at all strange if history came to the conclusion that the perfection of the bicycle was the greatest incident of the nineteenth century. ~ Detroit Tribune

- When man invented the bicycle he reached the peak of his attainments. Here was a machine of precision and balance for the convenience of man. And—unlike subsequent inventions for man's convenience—the more he used it, the fitter his body became. Here, for once, was a product of man's brain that was entirely beneficial to those who used it, and of no harm or irritation to others. Progress should have stopped when man invented the bicycle. ~ Elizabeth West

Board Games

- 2 Can Play at That Game
- Ahead of the Game
- Are You Game?
- Beating 'Em at Their Own Game
- Boardwalk's Mine! [Monopoly]
- Boggling My Rivals

- Bored Brains Need Board Games
- Checkmate!
- Colonel Mustard in the Billiards Room with the Wrench [Clue]
- Dice-y Prospects
- Did You Move My Piece?
- Fair Game
- "Frubry" is NOT a Word [Scrabble]
- Fun and Games
- The Game of Life
- The Game's Afoot
- Go Directly to Jail [Monopoly]
- Got Game?
- Home, Sweet Home
- I Accuse... [Clue]
- I'm Rich! [Monopoly]
- Just a Pawn in the Chess Game of Life
- King Me! [checkers]
- Long Live the King/Queen!
- The Mind Boggles [Boggle]
- My Favorite Pursuit [Trivial Pursuit]
- My Turn Next
- The Name of the Game

- No Cheating Zone
- The Only Game in Town
- Roll the Dice
- Scatter-brained [Scattergories]
- Serious Gamers
- Shoot! Chutes!
  [Chutes and Ladders]
- Snake Eyes
- This is My Game Face
- Triple Word Score! [Scrabble]
- We Got a Monopoly on Fun
- If life doesn't offer a game worth playing, then invent a new one. ~ Anthony J. D'Angelo
- When you see a good move, look for a better one. ~ Emanuel Lasker
- 'Tis all a checker-board of nights and days where destiny with men for pieces plays: Hither and thither moves, and mates and slays, and one by one back in the closet lays.
  ~ Omar Khayyam
- Risk is a part of God's game, alike for men and nations. ~ Warren Buffett
- Life is a kind of Chess, with struggle, competition, good and ill events.
  ~ Benjamin Franklin
- My computer beat me at checkers, but I sure beat it at kickboxing. ~ Emo Philips
- The only things I'm competitive in are backgammon and poker.
  ~ Kate Hudson
- The only athletic sport I ever mastered was backgammon.
  ~ Douglas William Jerrold
- To him, money was like the toy bank notes in Monopoly: he wanted it, not for what it could buy, but because it was needed to play the game. ~ Ken Follet
- I see the world more like checkers than chess.
  ~ Dennis Miller
- I like the moment when I break a man's ego. ~ Bobby Fischer
- Chess is a fairy tale of 1001 blunders. ~ Savielly Tartakower
- Chess is like war on a board. ~ Bobby Fischer
- Chess is played with the mind and not with the hands! ~ Renaud and Kahn
- The chess-board is the world, the pieces are the phenomena of the universe, the rules of the game are what we call the laws of nature. The player on the other side is hidden from us.
  ~ Thomas Henry Huxley

Boating

- [Michael], Row the Boat Ashore
- Ahoy Mateys
- All Aboard
- All is Calm, All is Bright
- All Wet
- Anchors Aweigh
- Any Port in a Storm
- As Much Use as a Handbrake on a Canoe
- As Still as Glass
- As They Sail Off into the Sunset
- Batten Down the Hatches
- The Big Wave
- Blue Water
- Boat Bums
- A Canoe for You
- Catch a Wave
- Catch the Wind
- Circumnavigate
- Come Aboard
- Come Sail Away
- Crazy about Kayaking
- Cross Currents
- Cruisin'
- A Day at the Races

- Dive Right In
- Don't Rock the Boat
- A Floatin' Party
- Full Steam Ahead
- Getting Their Feet Wet
- Go with the Flow
- H_2O
- He May Not be a God, but He Walks on Water
- I'd Rather be Sailing than Anything Else
- I'll be Sailing
- In Our Wake Better than in Our Sleep
- Just Add Water
- Kayaking the Night Away
- Kayakers are Smooth and Swift
- Land Lovers
- Land Lubbers
- Let's Sail Away
- Making a Splash!
- Making Waves
- Motoring
- A Need for Speed
- On Course and Full Steam
- Sails Ahead
- On the Waterfront

- On Your Mark, Get Set, Go!
- Out to Sea and Back Again
- Red Sails in the Sunset
- Ride the Wave
- Riding the Rapids
- Row, Row, Row Your Boat— Life is But a Dream
- Run Aground
- Sailing Away
- Sailing, Sailing over the Ocean Blue
- Sailing Takes Me Away
- The Sea of Love
- Shipwrecked
- Sittin' on the Dock and Wastin' Time
- Splash!
- Splish Splash
- Still Plays with Boats!
- Still Waters Run Deep
- Summer by the Sea
- Testing the Waters
- That Sinking Feeling
- Time and Tide Wait for No Man
- The Unsinkable [Molly Brown]
- Water Fest
- Water Wars

- Waterworld
- Wave Reviews
- Wet and Wild
- Whatever Floats Your Boat
- Where the Ocean Meets the Sky
- Whitewater
- Wishing You Calm Seas and a Gentle Breeze!
- You and Me by the Sea
- A lot of people ask me if I were shipwrecked, and could only have one book, what would it be? I always say How to Build a Boat.
  ~ Stephen Wright
- By the sea—by the sea—by the beautiful sea.
  ~ Harold Atteridge
- A ship in harbour is safe, but that is not what ships are built for. ~ William Shedd
- Everyone must believe in something. I believe I'll go canoeing. ~ Thoreau
- I grew up with boats on a lake we went to summers, but boating is one of the most tense ways to relax.
  ~ Andy Rooney
- Hoist up sail while gale doth last, Tide and wind stay no man's pleasure.
  ~ Robert Southwell

57

- Kayak polo's a good excuse to put on a skirt and play a sport.
  ~ Richard Shelton, on the waterproof skirt used during whitewater play

- There is no single toy Americans own so many of that they use so infrequently, as their boats. ~ Andy Rooney

- All I need is a tall ship and a star to sail her by.
  ~ John Masefeild

- Help thy brother's boat across, and Lo! thine own has reached the shore.
  ~ Hindu Proverb

- Although kayaking tends to draw a younger demographic, it is still a lifelong sport that anyone can get into. It's a sport anyone can enjoy, because it's not about strength, it's about technique.
  ~ Katherine Carr

- Definition: Boat (Bōt), n.- A hole in the water into which much money is thrown. ~ Unknown

- Believe me, my young friend, there is NOTHING—absolutely nothing—half so much worth doing as simply messing about in boats. ~ Kenneth Grahame

- The pessimist complains about the wind; the optimist expects it to change; the realist adjusts the sails.
  ~ William Arthur Ward

- Man cannot change the direction of the wind, but he can adjust his sails.
  ~ Unknown

- Let your boat of life be light, packed with only what you need. ~ Jerome K. Jerome

- People with the boat bug are never happier than when they are poking around marinas, fantasizing about owning other people's boats. It's a disease that costs more to cure than any other single common learning disability. ~ Randy Wayne White

- The water is the same on both sides of the boat.
  ~ Finnish Proverb

- The Owl and the Pussy-Cat went to sea in a beautiful pea-green boat...
  ~ Edward Lear

- Take everything as it comes; the wave passes, deal with the next one.
  ~ Tom Thomson

- Love many, trust a few, and always paddle your own canoe. ~ Bumper sticker

- No pessimist ever discovered the secrets of the stars, or sailed to an uncharted land, or opened a new heaven to the human spirit. ~ Helen Keller

- What sets a canoeing expedition apart is that it purifies you more rapidly and inescapably than any other travel. Travel a thousand miles by train and you are a brute; pedal five hundred on a bicycle and you remain basically a bourgeois; paddle a hundred in a canoe and you are already a child of nature. ~ Pierre Elliott Trudeau

- Only the guy who isn't rowing has time to rock the boat. ~ Jean-Paul Sartre

- So throw off the bowlines. Sail away from the safe harbor. Catch the trade winds in your sails. Explore. Dream. Discover. ~ Mark Twain

- You cannot sink someone else's end of the boat and still keep your own afloat.
  ~ Charles Bower

- On the ear drops the light drip of the suspended oar.
  ~ Lord Byron

- Never a ship sails out of bay but carries my heart as a stowaway.
  ~ Roselle Mercier Montgomery

- Originality is unexplored territory. You get there by carrying a canoe—you can't take a taxi. ~ Alan Alda

Bowling

- Bowler with an Attitude
- Bowlers Always Have Time to Spare
- Bowlers Don't Strike Out
- Bowlers Love to Strike Out
- Bowlers Never Die; They Just End Up in the Gutter
- Bowlers Prayer: Spare Us!
- Bowlers Strike Me as Special
- Bowling Bowls Me Over
- Bowling Green
- Bowling is a Ball
- Bowling is Right up My Alley!
- Chairmen of the Boards
- Great Turkey [3 strikes in a row]
- Grip It and Rip It
- Gutter Ball!
- Hat Trick [3 strikes in a row]
- Hitting the Lanes
- I Only Bowl on Days That End with Y
- I'm on a Drinking Team with a Bowling Problem

59

- King Pin
- Old Bowlers Never Die... They Just Don't Score as Much
- Split Happens!
- Strike It Up
- Strike!
- Ten in the Pit
- The Only Thing Going into the Gutter is My Mind
- They Wobble, but They Don't Fall Down
- Those Pins Have Round Bottoms!
- You Bowl Me Over
- The bowling alley is the poor man's country club.
  ~ Sanford Hansell
- I overcompensated too much.
  ~ Steven L. Bird, after failing to pick up a spare
- Heaven seems a little closer when your house is near the bowling ally. ~ Unknown
- We're going to be one big, happy, bowling family.
  ~ Sue Tenney
- Shopping tip: You can get shoes for a dollar at the bowling alley. ~ Unknown
- When you strike at a king, you must kill him.
  ~ Ralph Waldo Emerson

- One advantage of golf over bowling is that you never lose a bowling ball.
  ~ Don Carter
- I figured because I loved bowling so much, and I got started so late (in comparison to everyone else who was my age who bowled already), I would just make up for the last 8 or so years of not bowling, by bowling until my hand fell off. ~ Joe Tex
- We're not content with bowling for scores or awards, so we bowl for enlightenment. Strangely, to bowl for enlightenment, we bowl for scores and awards. ~ Eric Hew
- I was a little, skinny, runt kid, and I decided that bowling was what I was going to do in life.
  ~ Don Johnson
- I don't know what I'm doing, but I'm probably going to go bowling with all my girlfriends. ~ Drew Barrymore
- Practice, patience, and consistency all play big roles in racing and bowling. It doesn't matter what level player you are in bowling, you just laugh and have a great time. ~ Jeff Gordon

- Having a family is like having a bowling alley installed in your head.
  ~ Martin Mull

- The greats in bowling: Earl Anthony, Buzz Fazio, Ray Bluth, Dick Webber, Don Carter, Fred Flintstone.

Boxing

- Above the Belt, Please
- And in This Corner...
- Boxing Day
- Down But Not Out
- Down for the Count
- A Fighting Chance
- Heavyweight Champ
- I'll Handle Him/Her with Gloves... Prizefighting Gloves
- In the Ring
- Ka-Pow!
- Knockout!
- KO or O.K.?
- The Main Event
- My One-Two Punch
- No Holds Barred
- The Noble Art
- Not Ready to Throw in the Towel

- On the Ropes
- Out for the Count
- Queensbury Rules
- Real Lightweights are No Laughing Matter
- Ringside Seat
- Southpaw
- The Sweet Science
- That's a Low Blow!
- Taking It on the Chin
- Boxing, for me, it's the beginning of all sports. I'm willing to bet that the first sport was a man against another man in a fight, so I think that's something innate in all of us. ~ Omar Epps
- Boxing is show-business with blood.
  ~ David Belasco & Bruno Frank
- To me, boxing is like a ballet, except there's no music, no choreography, and the dancers hit each other. ~ Jack Handy
- Float like a butterfly, sting like a bee. ~ Muhammad Ali
- At home I am a nice guy- but I don't want the world to know. Humble people, I've found, don't get very far.
  ~ Muhammad Ali

- When archaeologists discover the missing arms of Venus de Milo, they will find she was wearing boxing gloves. ~ John Barrymore

- Attack is only one half of the art of boxing.
  ~ Georges Carpentier

- Champions aren't made in gyms. Champions are made from something they have deep inside them—a desire, a dream, a vision. They have to have last-minute stamina, they have to be a little faster, they have to have the skill and the will. But the will must be stronger than the skill.
  ~ Muhammad Ali

- Every time I hear the name Joe Louis my nose starts to bleed. ~ Tommy Farr

- It's just a job. Grass grows, birds fly, waves pound the sand. I beat people up. ~ Muhammad Ali

- Boxing should focus on pitting champion vs. champion. ~ Sugar Ray Leonard

- I coulda been a contenda.
  ~ Budd Schulberg

- Sure, there have been deaths and injuries in boxing, but none of them serious. ~ Alan Winter

- No one knows what to say in the loser's locker room.
  ~ Muhammad Ali

- There's nothing wrong with getting knocked down, as long as you get right back up. ~ Muhammad Ali

Camping

- Adventure Time
- All Spruced Up
- Back to Basics
- Back to Nature
- Bug Juice
- Campers Have S'more Fun!
- Campfire Cookin'
- Campfire Stories are the Greatest
- Campfire Storyteller
- Creepy Crawlers
- Cuddly Campers
- Escape to Nature
- Field and Stream
- "Field" Trip
- Fireside Chat
- Fireside Fun
- Give Me S'more Please
- Gone Campin'
- The Great Outdoors

SNAPPY SNIPPETS THAT SCORE!

- Happy Campers
- Hello Mada, Hello Fada, Here I am at Camp _____
- Home, Sweet Motor-home
- Home, Sweet Tent
- It's a 3-Dog Night
- It's a Cuddle Night Tonight
- Lovin' the Outdoors
- Nature: The Great Escape
- Roughing It!
- Rustic Wilderness
- Scout It Out
- S'more Great Moments
- Trail Blazers
- Under the Stars
- When in Doubt... Take a Hike
- Where There is Smoke, There is Fire
- The Wild Blue Yonder
- Wilderness Wise
- We didn't inherit the land from our fathers. We are borrowing it from our children. ~ An Amish Proverb
- It always rains on tents. Rainstorms will travel thousands of miles against prevailing winds for the opportunity to rain on a tent. ~ Dave Barry
- Sometimes it's a view without the room—and what a view.
- Camping: Nature's way of promoting the hotel industry. ~ Dave Barry
- Mighty oaks from tiny acorns grow. ~ Greek Proverb

Cards

- 52 Card Pick-Up
- Ace in the Hole
- Ace Up His/Her Sleeve
- The Bone Pile [nertz]
- Card Shark
- Crossing the Rubicon
- Deal 'Em, Cowboy
- Deuces Wild
- Dogs Playing Cards
- Full House
- Gin Rummy: Don't Knock It Till You've Tried It
- Go Fish!
- Golden Paw
- Got Any Twos?
- High Roller
- King/Queen of Hearts
- A Marriage Made in Heaven [pinochle]

63

- Maverick
- No Ace, No Face
- Not Playing with a Full Deck
- Up the Ante
- Raising the Stakes
- Shooting the Moon
- Spoon Fed [spoons]
- This is My Poker Face
- This Means War!
- When the Chips are Down
- Wild Card
- Old card players never die; they just shuffle away.
- Cards are war, in disguise of a sport. ~ Charles Lamb
- Each player must accept the cards life deals him or her: but once they are in hand, he or she alone must decide how to play the cards in order to win the game. ~ Voltaire
- I must complain the cards are ill shuffled till I have a good hand. ~ Jonathan Swift
- I could think of worse ways of going than at the poker table. ~ Al Alvarez
- I love blackjack. But I'm not addicted to gambling. I'm addicted to sitting in a semi-circle. ~ Mitch Hedberg
- Nobody is always a winner, and anybody who says he is, is either a liar or doesn't play poker. ~ Amarillo Slim
- If I lose today, I can look forward to winning tomorrow, and if I win today, I can expect to lose tomorrow. A sure thing is no fun. ~ Chico Marx
- The louder he talked of his honor, the faster we counted our spoons. ~ Ralph Waldo Emerson
- There are no friends at cards or world politics. ~ Finley Peter Dunne
- Coaches are an integral part of any manager's team, especially if they are good pinochle players. ~ Earl Weaver
- Over the years, people taught me all kinds of other card games: Spades; Hearts; Whist; O'Pshaw; Pinochle; Canasta. I've forgotten most of them because they turned out to be pale subsets of Bridge, more or less. I was never inclined to become a Bridge master, but it was clearly the granddaddy of them all and the only one that would hold interest in the long run for a serious player. ~ Clifford Beshers

- The smarter you play, the luckier you'll be. ~ Mark Pilarski

- Blackjack is the only casino game an amateur can learn to play and at which he can definitely win. ~ Lawrence Revere

- I believe in poker the way I believe in the American Dream. Poker is good for you. It enriches the soul, sharpens the intellect, heals the spirit, and—when played well, nourishes the wallet. ~ Lou Krieger

- Thou shalt not complaineth about the cards the Lord thy Euchre God hath bestowed upon ye. ~ Lapp

- Trust everybody, but cut the cards. ~ Finley Peter Dunne

- The commonest mistake in history is underestimating your opponent; it happens at the poker table all the time. ~ David Shoup

- Poker's the only game fit for a grown man. Then, your hand is against every man's, and every man's is against yours. Teamwork? Who ever made a fortune by teamwork? There's only one way to make a fortune, and that's to down the fellow who's up against you. ~ W. Somerset Maugham

- Poker is to cards and games what jazz is to music. It's this great American thing, born and bred here. We dig it because everybody can play. ~ Steve Lipscomb

- Last night I stayed up late playing poker with Tarot cards. I got a full house and four people died. ~ Steven Wright

Cheerleading

- 2, 4, 6, 8—Who Do We Appreciate?

- Athlete by Nature, Cheerleader by Choice

- Be Calm, be Cool, and be Collected—Hey Hey!

- The Best Team in the West

- Bringing in the School Spirit

- C-H-E-E-R!

- The Chain is Only as Strong as the Weakest Link

- Cheer All Out or Don't Cheer at All

- Cheer My Way Through

- Cheer My Way Through College? Watch Me!

- Cheer the Game! Work the

- Crowd! Build the Spirit!

- Cheer Them to a Win!
- A Cheerleader is a Dreamer Who Never Gives Up
- Cheerleaders are a Team and There is No "I" in Team!
- Cheerleaders are Expected to be Loud!
- Cheerleading is More Than a Sport; It's an Attitude
- Cheerleading is My Obsession
- Cheerleading is the Passion for Perfection!
- Cheerleading Makes Me Jump and Shout
- Competition Bound
- Defense! Defense!
- Eat. Sleep. Cheer. Repeat.
- Extend Yourself—Cheer
- Flying isn't Just for the Birds Anymore!
- Give Me a [first letter of school name]!
- Go Blue! [School Colors]
- Go Team, Fight Team, Win Team, Win!
- Go, Fight, Win
- Go, Team, Go
- Hey, There is No Halftime for Cheerleaders!
- Hold That Line
- Home Team Advantage
- Hooray for Our Team
- I Don't Just Cheer—I Inspire
- I Don't Play the Field—I Rule the Sidelines.
- I Only Cheer on Two Occasions: Day and Night
- I Sleep, I Dream, I Cheer
- If Cheerleading was Easy, It Would be Called Football
- If It's in Your Heart, It Shows in Your Spirit
- If You've Got the Game, We've Got the Cheer
- I'll Fly Away
- I'm Not a Cheerleader—I'm an Athletic Supporter
- Jocks Lift Weights... Cheerleaders Lift People!
- Jump, Shout, Knock Yourself Out!
- Jump, Shout, Yell!
- Let's Go!
- Live to Cheer!
- Look at Her Fly
- Nothing's Sweeter Than This Cheerleader!
- On the Top of the World {pyramid]
- Pep Rally

- Pom-Poms 'R' Us
- Pom-Poms and Ponytails
- Push 'Em Back, Push 'Em Back, Waaaaay Back
- Pyramid Scheme
- Rah-Rah, Siss Boom Bah
- Stand Up and Cheer
- Team Up
- There is Only One Way to Cheer—Hard!
- There's More to Life Than Just Cheering... Yeah Right!
- The Time to Cheer is Near!
- Today's Heroes
- We are the Champions... We are the Champions
- We've Got the Spirit!
- Wimps Lift Weights, Cheerleaders Lift People
- Without Cheerleaders, It's Only a Game
- Yay, Team!
- You Let Us Win Like We Let You Lose!
- You Lift Me High
- You Make the Touchdown, We'll Make the Noise!
- You Mess with Me, You Mess with the Whole Squad
- A good cheerleader is not measured by the height of her jumps but by the span of her spirit. ~ Unknown
- Cheerleading is not what it used to be. It's no longer standing on the sidelines looking cute in a skirt. ~ Erin Brooks
- All women are created equal, then a few become cheerleaders.
- Cheer—ability is a talent for deciding something quickly and getting everyone in the stadium doing it. ~ Unknown
- If you want to compete... practice. If you want to win... practice harder
- Trust is the biggest factor in cheerleading; you have to trust the people under you ... Any guy can hold her hand, but it takes the elite to hold her feet. ~ Taylor Clark
- Cheerleaders are angels. We're the only humans who can fly.
- In any other sport, if you miss the catch all you lose is the ball.
- If she cheers, chants, flips, tumbles, yells, stunts, jumps or just plain has spirit, she's a cheerleader!

- Cheerleaders are not just friends, they are family! They support one another everyday through smiles and encouraging words. They have a special bond that can never be broken.
  ~ Unknown

- It's not the glitz of the uniform that matters, but the spirit that shines within it.

- Root, root, root for the home team... if they don't win it's a shame.
  ~ Jack Norworth

- Cheerleaders are the only ones who know how to fly high and reach their goals at the same time.

- Cheerleaders know that pyramids were not built in Egypt.

- Flying is the second best thrill to cheerleaders; being caught is the first.

- I run like a girl, jump like a girl, and pop 10 feet into the air like a girl!

- I trade sweat for strength. I trade doubt for belief. I trade cheerleading for nothing.

- If football is so spectacular, why does it take cheerleaders to excite the crowd?

- Cheerleaders are simply a jump above the rest.

- Just because we don't run across goal lines, slam dunk basketballs or hit homeruns doesn't mean we can't change the score!

- Cheer shoes: $75. Cheer camp: $200. Winning your first national competition—priceless!

- Cheerleading is very athletic, there's no doubt about that, but the main purpose remains the same, to generate spirit, lead the crowd. ~ Jeff Webb

- It doesn't matter if you win or lose the game—it's how loud you cheer!

- Players—a vital part of any sporting event, they entertain the crowd in the intervals between timeouts so the cheerleaders can take a well-earned break.

- The only difference between us and ball players is we jump, toss, and catch year round.

- The spirit to win and the will to succeed are measured one stunt at a time.

- You may think you're all that, but you can't get anywhere without your squad.

- The referees have always been blind, it's our job to make them deaf.
- There are two types of people in this world: cheerleaders and those who wish they were!
- Peace, love, and cheerleading. The rest is just details.
- What is cheerleading competition? A sports event consisting entirely of 3 minute timeouts.
  ~ Unknown
- It's hard to be humble when you can jump, stunt, and tumble!
- What you see is what you get, and you ain't seen nothin' yet!
- You know you're a cheerleader when you have to yell, kick and scream to get what you want.
- There is no team, like the best team, which is our team, right here.
- Yes, I'm a cheerleader, yes, I'm an athlete, yes, I'm a girl... You gotta problem with that?
- Together we stand, together we fall. All for one... and one for all!

Childhood Games

- All Tied Up [yo-yo, jump rope]
- Ashes, Ashes, We All Fall Down!
- At the End of My Tether [tetherball]
- The Bone Pile [dominos]
- Clap Trap [clapping games]
- Cinderella, Dressed in Yella... [jump rope]
- Come Out, Come Out, Wherever You Are!
- Destroyer Sunk! [battleship]
- The Domino Effect
- Duck, Duck, GOOSE!
- In Full Swing
- In the Swing of Things
- Jump for Joy [jump rope]
- Know the Ropes [jump rope]
- Losing His/Her Marbles
- Low Man on the Tetherball Pole
- Miss Mary Mack, Mack, Mack... [clapping games]
- Monkey in the Middle
- Olly Olly Oxen Free
- On the Ropes [jump rope]
- Onesies and Twosies [jacks]
- Playing for Keeps [marbles]

69

- POP! Goes the Weasel
- Red Light! Green Light!
- Red Rover, Red Rover, Send _____ Right Over
- Ring Around the Rosie
- Roped In [jump rope]
- One Word, Sounds Like... [charades]
- Tag! You're It!
- Yo! [yo-yo]
- One thing I did with my dad, which was very dramatic, was play outdoor hide-and-seek. We would play with grown-ups, and they took it so seriously.
  ~ Ashley Judd
- Laser tag is a great team building tool. ~ Franco Carofano
- One of life's primal situations; the game of hide and seek. Oh, the delicious thrill of hiding while the others come looking for you, the delicious terror of being discovered, but what panic when, after a long search, the others abandon you! You mustn't hide too well. You mustn't be too good at the game. The player must never be bigger than the game itself.
  ~ Jean Baudrillard
- There's less violence in the world when people are using Hula-Hoops. ~ Mikey Way
- Laser tag isn't just for kids; it's for adults too.
  ~ Franco Carofano
- Hopscotch, it was bizarre for boys, 'cause they never played it, and as a boy, I was behind walls, going, "What—what happened? What did they do? What do they do here?" And they had a track laid out with numbers, mystic numbers— 1, 5... 7, 8, you know... A bit of a broken doll there, some girl keeping lookout with a skipping rope...
  ~ Eddie Izzard
- Of course I have played outdoor games. I once played dominoes in an open air cafe in Paris.
  ~ Oscar Wilde

Climbing

- Are You in a Good Spot?
- Be Sharp or be Flat
- Beta Max or Heavy Racks
- Climb On
- Climbers Rock!
- Crank the Edge or Hit the Ledge

70

- Defying Gravity
- Don't be a Moper; Reach for the Sloper
- Finger Locks or Cedar Box
- Flash Man or Trash Can
- Hand Jam or Test Cam
- Hang On Tight!
- If You Fail to Prepare, Prepare to Fail
- If You Fail to Prevail, Prepare to Impale
- Mohammad Comes to the Mountain
- Mountaintop Experience
- Move That Hold, You're Growing Mold
- Off to a Rocky Start
- On Belay
- When in Doubt, Run It Out
- I don't want to write about climbing; I don't want talk about it; I don't want to photograph it; I don't want to think about it; all I want to do is do it.
  ~ Chuck Pratt
- You climb for the hell of it.
  ~ Edmund Hillary
- I think you love rocks so much that they've replaced your brain. ~ Rex Pieper

- The best climber in the world is the one who's having the most fun.
  ~ Alex Lowe
- When you get to the end of your rope, tie a knot and hang on.
  ~ Franklin D. Roosevelt
- I've climbed with some of the best climbers in the world, more importantly, to me, they are some of the best people in the world. That's another reason why I climb.
  ~ Jim Wickwire
- Because it is there.
  ~ George Mallory
- I've tried many sports, but climbing is the best. The beauty of this sport is that no matter how good you get, you can always find a way to challenge yourself. ~ Randy Leavitt
- There are only three real sports: bull-fighting, car racing and mountain climbing. All the others are mere games. ~ Hemingway
- Some of the world's greatest feats were accomplished by people not smart enough to know they were impossible.
  ~ Doug Lawson

Coaching

- Because I'm the Coach— That's Why
- Coach and Four
- Coaches are Good Sports!
- Coaches Get a Kick out of Life!
- Coaching: A Lot of People Doing What I Say
- Coffee & Coach Don't Mix
- Come Prepared to Win
- Don't Make Me Use My Coaching Voice!
- Give It Your Best
- GO GO GO!
- Hit the Showers
- Hustle!
- I Didn't Come Here to Lose
- I Want 110%
- If Coach Ain't Happy, Ain't Nobody Happy
- Keep Your Head in the Game
- Let's Go, Team!
- Look Alive Out There!
- No Pain, No Gain
- Put Me In, Coach!
- Save the Drama for Your Mama

- Thanks, Coach
- This is a No Whine Zone
- Whatever You Do, Don't Make Coach Cry
- Whistle-Blower
- You Can't Scare Me—I'm a Coach!
- You've Gotta Want It
- I told him, "Son, what is it with you? Is it ignorance or apathy?" He said, "Coach, I don't know and I don't care." ~ Frank Layden
- A good coach will make his players see what they can be rather than what they are. ~ Ara Parasheghian
- Discipline and demand without being demeaning. ~ Don Meyer
- Either love your players or get out of coaching. ~ Bobby Dodd
- A successful coach needs a patient wife, loyal dog and great quarterback—and not necessarily in that order. ~ Bud Grant
- A tough day at the office is even tougher when your office contains spectator seating. ~ Nik Posa
- Coaches build teams, parents build players. ~ Charles Smyth

- Coaches have to watch for what they don't want to see and listen to what they don't want to hear. ~ John Madden

- Coaches who can outline plays on a blackboard are a dime a dozen. The one's who win get inside their players and motivate. ~ Vince Lombardi

- In a crisis, don't hide behind anything or anybody. They are going to find you anyway. ~ Paul "Bear" Bryant

- Coaching is a profession of love. You can't coach people unless you love them. ~ Eddie Robinson

- I'd rather be a football coach. That way you can lose only 11 games a season. I lost 11 games in December alone! ~ Abe Lemons

- He treats us like men. He lets us wear earrings. ~ Torrin Polk, on Coach Jenkins

- What makes a good coach? Complete dedication. ~ George Halas

- I never questioned the integrity of an umpire. Their eyesight, yes. ~ Leo Durocher

- Over-coaching is the worst thing you can do to a player. ~ Dean Smith

- Coaching is making men do what they don't want so they can become what they want to be. ~ Tom Landry

- If a coach starts listening to fans, he winds up sitting next to them. ~ Johnny Kerr

- Coaching is not a natural way of life. Your victories and losses are too clear cut. ~ Tommy Prothro

- I knew we were in for a long season when we lined up for the national anthem on opening day and one of my players said, "Every time I hear that song I have a bad game." ~ Jim Leyland

- I learn teaching from teachers. I learn golf from golfers. I learn winning from coaches. ~ Harvey Penick

- If anything goes bad, I did it. If anything goes semi-good, we did it. If anything goes really good, then you did it. That's all it takes to get people to win football games for you. ~ Paul "Bear" Bryant

- It's a very bad thing to become accustomed to good luck. ~ Publilius Syrus

- Kids don't care how much you know, until they know how much you care. ~ Unknown

- If it doesn't matter who wins or loses, then why do they keep score? ~ Vince Lombardi

- Good coaching may be defined as the development of character, personality and habits of players, plus the teaching of fundamentals and team play. ~ Claire Bee

- Leadership, like coaching, is fighting for the hearts and souls of men and getting them to believe in you. ~ Eddie Robinson

- Sport doesn't teach character, coaches teach character. ~ Unknown

- You can motivate by fear, and you can motivate by reward. But both those methods are only temporary. The only lasting thing is self-motivation. ~ Homer Rice

- The trouble with referees is that they know the rules, but they do not know the game.
  ~ Bill Shankly, manager

- Make sure that team members know they are working with you, not for you. ~ John Wooden

- Other people go to the office. I get to coach. I know I've been blessed.
  ~ Jim Valvano

- My responsibility is leadership, and the minute I get negative, that is going to have an influence on my team. ~ Don Shula

- Officials are the only guys who can rob you and then get a police escort out of the stadium. ~ Ron Bolton

- Luck is what happens when preparation meets opportunity. ~ Darrell Royal

- Professional coaches measure success in rings. College coaches measure success in championships. High school coaches measure success in titles. Youth coaches measure success in smiles.
  ~ Paul Mcallister

- The coach should be the absolute boss, but he still should maintain an open mind. ~ Red Auerbach

- The most important quality I look for in a player is accountability. You've got to be accountable for who you are. It's too easy to blame things on someone else. ~ Lenny Wilkins

- The secret to winning is constant, consistent management. ~ Tom Landry

Cricket

- All Out
- Batsman and Rabbit
- Bail Me Out
- Bowled Over
- Crazy Cricket
- Cricket Addict
- Duh Da, Duh Da, Batsman!
- Hat Trick
- Howzat?
- Red Cherries
- Overs and Out
- Sticky Wicket
- That's Just Not Cricket
- Wicked Wicket
- I do love cricket — it's so very English. ~ Sarah Bernhardt
- Cricket: If it were easy, they'd call it "baseball."
- Cricket makes no sense to me. I find it beautiful to watch, and I like that they break for tea. That is very cool, but I don't understand. ~ Jim Jarmusch
- But I always knew I would excel in cricket. ~ Imran Khan
- Cricket was my reason for living. ~ Harold Larwood

- If the French noblesse had been capable of playing cricket with their peasants, their chateaux would never have been burnt. ~ G. M. Trevelyan
- You can cut the tension with a cricket stump. ~ Murray Walker
- Baseball and cricket are beautiful and highly stylized medieval war substitutes, chess made flesh, a mixture of proud chivalry and base—in both senses—greed. ~ John Fowles
- Cricket to us was more than play, it was a worship in the summer sun. ~ Edmund Blunden
- I tend to think that cricket is the greatest thing that God ever created on earth. ~ Harold Pinter

Croquet

- Croquet Anyone?
- Going Through Hoops
- If You Can't Roquet, You Can't Croquet
- Mallet Mad
- Snake in the Grass
- Start the Ball Rolling

- Sticky Wicket
- Wicked Wickets
- You Wicket Thing!
- The temptation to misuse these things is awful.
  ~ Bill Watterson, on mallets
- It's like pool, except you're standing on the table.
  ~ Jerry Stark
- That's the best part of the game. You get to launch the other guy's ball into oblivion and take another turn. ~ Bill Amend
- Croquet is tough. People play for months because the rules are so bizarre. Those crazy English.
  ~ Jane Kaczmarek
- It combines chess, pool and war—because it is a war out there. It's blood and guts, but you don't see it spilled on the ground.
  ~ Jerry Stark

Curling

- Broad Brush Strokes
- The Brush Off
- Brushing Up on My Technique
- Cast the First Stone
- Clean Sweep
- Curlers Clean House

- Man/Woman of the House
- Rock On!
- Rock the House
- Rockin' and Rollin'
- Sweep Me Away
- Swept Off My Feet
- When hell freezes over, I'll curl there too. ~ T-shirt
- People who live in ice houses can throw all the stones they want.
- Curlers bring the house down.
- Curling teams pick their own players. You have to be able to play with people you get along with on and off the ice. We like to think of ourselves as equals out there. Each of us could play any position. Our philosophy is simple—be patient on the ice and have fun. ~ Cassie Johnson
- Curlers are always just a stone's throw from the house.
- If curling were easy, they'd call it hockey.
- Curling is sweeping the nation.
- Curling is a very interesting sport because it's like shuffleboard on ice.
  ~ Adam West

76

Dance

- All She Wants to Do is Dance
- All That Jazz
- Another Shirley Temple
- Attitude Dancing
- Baby, Take a Bow
- Ballet Keeps Me on My Toes
- Bee Bop [bee embellishments]
- Belle of the Ball
- Best of Show
- Boogie Down
- Boogie Fever
- Bop Till You Drop
- Break a Leg
- Bravo! Encore!
- Care to Dance?
- Catch a Rising Star
- Cloggin'
- D A N C E
- Dance Allows Your Dreams to Speak
- Dance Dreams
- Dance Dynamics
- Dance Electric
- Dance Fever
- Dance into the Night
- Dance Like Nobody's Watching
- The Dance of the Sugarplum Fairies
- Dance or Die!
- Dance Smoothes the Rough Edges of Life
- Dance until the Cows Come Home
- Dance to Live or Live to Dance?
- Dance to the Music
- Dance, Dance, Dance
- Dance, Dance. Prance, Prance—That's My Life!
- Dancer Dreams
- Dancer with an Attitude
- Dancers "Turnout" Better!
- Dancers Have Attitude
- Dancers Have the Best Buns!
- Dances with Wolves
- Dancin' Feet
- Dancing Duo
- Dancing Queen
- Dancing Toes
- Do a Little Dance
- Do the Hustle
- Dressed to Dance
- Fancy Footwork
- Feet Don't Fail Me Now

- Flash Dance
- Future Ballerina
- Go for It! Life is Not a Dress Rehearsal!
- Got My Dancing Shoes on
- Gotta Dance
- Happy Feet
- Havin' a Ball, Y'all
- Hip Hop
- Hippy, Hippy Shake
- Hit Your Mark
- Hoof It
- I Brake for Dancers
- I Dance, Therefore I am
- I Love to Dance
- I'm Dancing as Fast as I Can!
- It's All about Barre-work!
- I've Got Rhythm
- Jazzing
- Jitterbug Girl
- Just Dance
- Keep on Dancin'
- Keeping on Their Toes
- Let's Boogie
- Let's Celebrate!
- Let's Dance
- Life is Simple. Eat. Sleep.
Dance!
- Lord of the Dance
- Making Strides by Leaps and Bounds
- Mr. Bo Jangles
- Neutron Dance
- Once a Dancer, Always a Dancer
- One Good Turn Deserves Another
- Our Shining Star(s)
- Practice Makes Perfect
- Put on Your Dancin' Shoes
- Puttin' On The Ritz
- Recital
- River Dance
- Shake It Up, Baby
- Shake That Bootie
- Shimmy Shake
- Shoot for the Stars
- Something in the Way She Moves
- Stage Door Groupies
  [Mom and Dad]
- Star Quality
- Step by Step
- Steppin' Out
- Stomp

- Superstar
- Take Center Stage
- Takes Two to Tango
- Tappin'
- The Show Must Go on
- Time to Tap
- Tiny Dancer
- To Dance or Not to Dance? Silly Question.
- To Tap or Not to Tap? Silly Question.
- Tuxedo Function/Junction
- Twinkle Toes
- Twist and Shout!
- Up on Their Toes
- We've Got Rhythm
- Why Walk when You Can Dance?
- You are Tu-Tu Cute!
- Dance is a song of the body. ~ Martha Graham
- Creativity takes courage! ~ Henry Matisse
- Dancers are instruments, like a piano the choreographer plays. ~ George Balanchine
- Remember, Ginger Rogers did everything Fred Astaire did, but backwards and in high heels. ~ Faith Whittlesey

- Dancing is the only art of which we ourselves are the stuff of which it is made. ~ Ted Shawn
- Dance like there's nobody watching, love like you'll never get hurt, sing like there's nobody listening, live like it's heaven on earth. ~ William Purkey
- Everyday I count wasted in which there has been no dancing. ~ Nietzche
- Dance to the music of your dreams; the steps will bring you joy.
- Dance is the hidden language of the soul. ~ Martha Graham
- A dignified and formal dance is a delicately planned geometry. ~ Ruth Katz
- Your feet may hurt, your hair coming uncurled, but it's a great feeling when you collect the prize you've earned. ~ Irish dancer's saying
- Dance: If it were easy, It would be called "football."
- Dance is a sort of silent rhetoric. ~ Canon Thoinot Arbeau
- Dance in the body you have and make it the best you've ever done. ~ Agnes Demille
- If all the world's a stage, I want better lighting.

- If the dance is right, there shouldn't be a single superfluous movement. ~ Fred Astaire
- If you can talk, you can sing. If you can walk, you can dance. ~ African Proverb
- Dancers are the athletes of God. ~ Albert Einsten
- If you're going to walk on thin ice, you might as well dance! ~ Unknown
- Music is an invisible dance, as dancing is silent music. ~ Unknown
- Artists lead unglamorous daily lives of discipline and routine, but their work is full of passion. Each has a vision and feels responsibility to that vision. ~ Merryl Brockway
- Never criticize your dance partner. ~ Brave Combo
- The dance is the mother of all languages. ~ R.G. Collingwood
- What if the hokey pokey is really what it's all about?
- There's no business like show business. ~ Ethel Merman
- Those who dance are thought mad by those who hear not the music. ~ Unknown
- Twistin' the night away. ~ Sam Cooke

Darts

- A Cock-and-Bull's-Eye Story
- Back to the Old Dartboard
- Beat That, Robin Hood!
- Chairman/woman of the Dartboard
- Darts Players are Always on Board
- Darting Away
- Diddle for the Middle
- Full of Bull's Eyes
- Hat Trick
- I was Aiming for the Wall!
- Put a Cork in It
- Shooting the Bull
- Spray 'n' Pray
- Sweep the Board
- Take the Bull's Eye by the Horns
- Throw a Fit
- Throw Caution to the Wind
- Laughter winged his polished dart... ~ William Winters
- His darts used to stick out like tulips in the board. ~ Bobby George
- That was like throwing three pickled onions into a thimble! ~ Sid Waddell

- All you need to play professional darts is a loud shirt that you don't tuck into your trousers, a stomach the size of Staffordshire and an idiotic nickname.
  ~ Jeremy Clarkson

- How hard thy yoke, how cruel thy dart. ~ Matthew Prior

- There's only one word for that—magic darts!
  ~ Sid Waddell

- A feeble dart short of its mark. ~ Virgil

Equestrian

- All the Pretty Little Horses
- Airs above the Ground
- Black Beauty
- Born to Ride
- Care, Not Fine Stables, Makes a Good Horse
- Catch as Catch Can
- Canter Banter
- Center Field
- Daily Double
- Easy Rider
- English Proper
- Giddy-Up
- Gone Ridin'

- Happy Trails to You
- High Roller
- Hitching Post 10 Cents... the Reins Stop Here
- Hobby: Horses
- Home, Sweet Barn
- The Horse is God's Gift to Man
- Horse Lovers are Stable People
- Horse Parkin'
- Horse Play
- Horse Sense is Only Stable Thinking
- Horse with No Name
- Horses are Predictably Unpredictable
- Horsey, Horsey, on Your Way
- Horsin' Around
- Knight on a White Horse
- Lean into the Jump
- The Mane Event
- Pony Tales
- Ride like the Wind
- Run for the Roses
- The Sport of Kings
- Tally Ho!
- Thoroughbred

- To Ride a Horse is to Ride the Sky
- Un-Easy Rider
- Warm-Up Romp
- Wild Horses
- Win—Place—Show
- A Woman's Place: On a Horse
- It is not enough for a man to know how to ride; he must know how to fall.
  ~ Mexican Proverb
- A horse is worth more than riches. ~ Spanish Proverb
- To me, horses and freedom are synonymous.
  ~ Veryl Goodnight
- Don't look a gift horse in the mouth.
- When I bestride him, I soar, I am a hawk: he trots the air; the earth sings when he touches it; the basest horn of his hoof is more musical than the pipe of Hermes. ~ Shakespeare
- The wind of heaven is that which blows between a horse's ears. ~ Arabian Proverb
- A horse is a thing of such beauty ... none will tire of looking at him as long as he displays himself in his splendor. ~ Xenophon
- God forbid that I should go to any heaven in which there are no horses.
  ~ R.B. Cunningham Graham
- A man on a horse is spiritually as well as physically bigger than a man on foot. ~ John Steinbeck
- Every time you ride, your either teaching or un-teaching your horse.
  ~ Gordon Wright
- A canter is a cure for every evil. ~ Benjamin Disraeli
- When Allah created the horse, he said to the wind ... "Condense thyself." And the wind condensed itself, and the result was the horse. ~ Marguerite Henry
- They are more beautiful than anything in the world, kinetic sculpture, perfect form in motion. ~ Kate Millet
- Don't put the cart before the horse.
- And I looked, and beheld a pale horse: and his name that sat upon him was death. ~ Revelations 6:8
- It is the difficult horses that have the most to give you. ~ Lendon Gray
- Be wary of the horse with a sense of humor. ~ Pam Brown

- God first made man. He thought better of it and made woman. When he had time, he made the horse, which has the courage and spirit of man and the beauty and grace of woman. ~ Brazilian Saying

- Don't change horses in the middle of the stream.

- All horses deserve, at least once in their lives, to be loved by a little girl. ~ Unknown

- Horse sense is the thing a horse has which keeps it from betting on people.
  ~ W. C. Fields

- He's the kind of horse with a far-away look. He'll sure take a man through some awful places and sometimes only one comes out.
  ~ WS James

- Horses lend us the wings we lack. ~ Pam Brown

- How do you catch a loose horse? Make a noise like a carrot. ~ British cavalry joke

- In riding a horse we borrow freedom. ~ Helen Thomson

- Judge not the horse by his saddle. ~ Chinese proverb

- One man's wrong lead is another man's counter-canter. ~ S.D. Price

- Thou shall fly without wings and conquer without a sword. ~ Koran

- It excites me that no matter how much machinery replaces the horse, the work it can do is still measured in horsepower...even in this space age. And although a riding horse often weighs half a ton, and a big drafter a full ton, either can be led about by a piece of string if he has been wisely trained. This to me is a constant source of wonder, and challenge.
  ~ Marguret Henry

- Hitching a hackney pony to the Budweiser wagon won't make him a Clydesdale.

- Horses make any landscape look beautiful.
  ~ Alice Walker

- My husband said if I didn't sell my horses, he would leave me. Some days I really miss him.

- No hour of life is wasted that is spent in the saddle.
  ~ Winston Churchill

- If your horse says no, you either asked the wrong question or asked the question wrong. ~ Pat Parelli

- One reason why birds and horses are happy is because they are not trying to impress other birds and horses. ~ Dale Carnegie

- Our greatest glory is not in never falling, but in rising every time we fall. ~ Confucius

- The essential joy of being with horses is that it brings us in contact with the rare elements of grace, beauty, spirit and fire. ~ Sharon Ralls Lemon

- How do you stop this crazy thing?! ~ George Jetson

- Never trust a cowhand that doesn't know how to properly tie a horse.

- When taking a wife or buying a horse, close your eyes and command yourself to God. ~ Spanish Saying

- The knowledge of the nature of a horse is one of the first foundations of the art of riding it, and every horseman must make it his principal study. ~ Francois de la Guérinière

- The wildest colts make the best horses. ~ Plutarch

- You cannot train a horse with shouts and expect it to obey a whisper. ~ Dagobert D. Runes

- There is no secret as that between a rider and his horse. ~ Robert Surtees

- You can tell a gelding, you can ask a stallion, but you must discuss it with a mare.

- There are only two emotions that belong in the saddle; one is a sense of humour and the other is patience. ~ John Lyons

- There is something about the outside of a horse that is good for the inside of a man. ~ Winston Churchill

- There's something in riding a fine horse that can make a man feel more than mortal.

- Understanding the soul of a horse is the closest we humans can come to knowing perfection. ~ Unknown

- You and your horse: His strength and beauty, your knowledge and patience and determination and understanding and love. That's what fuses the two of you into this marvelous partnership that makes you wonder, what can heaven offer any better than what you have here on earth? ~ Monica Dickens

Fans

- #1 Fan
- The Agony of Defeat
- Biggest Fans
- Bleacher Bums
- Cheering 'n' Jeering
- Do the Wave
- Fanatic Fans
- Fanning the Flames
- Forever Fans
- From the Bleachers
- GO Team!
- Got [favorite team, driver, player, etc.]?
- I Bleed [team colors]
- It's All Over But the Crying
- It's All Over But the Shouting
- Just One More Inning/Lap/Quarter/Etc.
- More Than a Spectator
- MVF: Most Valuable Fan
- My Team's Better Than Your Team!
- No Fair-Weather Fan
- No, I'm Not a Fan—I Just Really Hate the Other Team
- Official Member of the _____ Fan Club
- Paint the Town _____ [team colors]
- Painted Ladies
- Root, Root, Root for the Home Team
- Sporting the Team Colors
- Tailgate Kings
- That's Gotta Hurt!
- We Will Rock You!
- OK, he's a Yankees fan. Now I know why I don't like him. ~ Dave Winer
- Sharks are as tough as those football fans who take their shirts off during games in Chicago in January, only more intelligent. ~ Dave Barry
- Being a sports fan is a complex matter, in part irrational but not unworthy a relief from the seriousness of the real world, with its unending pressures and often grave obligations. ~ Richard Gilman
- Anyone can support a team that is winning—it takes no courage. But to stand behind a team, to defend a team when it is down and really needs you, that takes a lot of courage. ~ Bart Starr

- As the game enters its glorious final weeks, the chill of fall signals the reality of defeat for all but one team. The fields of play will turn brown and harden, the snow will fall, but in the heart of the fan sprouts a sprig of green. ~ John Thorn

- I'm not a big sports fan, but I love it when they "slam dunk." That's sexy.
  ~ Emma Bunton

- A rabid sports fan is one that boos a TV set.
  ~ Jimmy Cannon

- The reason sport is attractive to many of the general public is that it's filled with reversals. What you think may happen doesn't happen. A champion is beaten, an unknown becomes a champion. ~ Roger Bannister

- The natural state of the football fan is bitter disappointment, no matter what the score. ~ Nick Hornby

- Fans don't boo nobodies.
  ~ Reggie Jackson

- All literary men are Red Sox fans—to be a Yankee fan in a literate society is to endanger your life.
  ~ John Cheever

- If you're a sports fan you realize that when you meet somebody, like a girlfriend, they kind of have to root for your team. They don't have a choice. ~ Jimmy Fallon

- I left because of illness and fatigue. The fans were sick and tired of me.
  ~ John Ralston

- The sentimentality of baseball is very deeply rooted in the American baseball fan. It is the one sport that is transmitted from fathers to sons.
  ~ Michael Lewis

- I'm still a huge fan. I love the game, and probably even more so now that they throw the ball every down. I'm envious.
  ~ Steve Largent

- We picked the Red Sox because they lose. If you root for something that loses for 86 years, you're a pretty good fan. You don't have to win everything to be a fan of something. ~ Jimmy Fallon

- One thing you learned as a Cubs fan: when you bought your ticket, you could bank on seeing the bottom of the ninth. ~ Joe Garagiola

- The fan is the one who suffers. He cheers a guy to a .350 season then watches that player sign with another team. When you destroy fan loyalties, you destroy everything.
  ~ Frank Robinson

- Anyone with any real blood in his or her veins cannot help being a fan. Being a true American and being a fan are synonymous.
  ~ Lulu Glaser

- Miranda was a huge fan of the Yankees. I was a huge fan of being anywhere you could smoke and drink at two in the afternoon without judgment.
  ~ Sex in the City

Fencing

- Attack!
- Armed and Dangerous
- Armed Assault
- At Sword's Point
- Come to the Point
- Crossed Swords
- Duel to the Death
- Eat Your Heart Out, Hamlet!
- En Garde!
- Fencing: Get the Point?

- Fencing is My Strong Point
- Fencing: Show a Little Flèche
- Fight Like the Devil, Die Like a Gentleman
- Foiled Again!
- Getting Right to the Point
- Hot Sweat and Cold Steel
- On Guard!
- On the Fence
- Parret and Thrust
- Pleasures of the Flèche
- Pointed Remarks
- Robin Hood, Eat Your Heart Out!
- Running with Sharp Objects
- Sabre Rattling
- Sword Play
- Swords Never Run Out of Bullets
- Taking the Lunge
- The Three Musketeers Got Nothing on Me
- Thrust and Parry
- Touché!
- Warning: Addictive Sport— May Contain Swords
- Will Fence for Food
- Zorro in Training

- The pen is mightier than the sword if the sword is very short, and the pen is very sharp. ~ Terry Pratchett

- Fencing made me feel for the first time like a winner. ~ Neil Diamond

- Remember that when you meet your antagonist, to do everything in a mild agreeable manner. Let your courage be keen, but at the same time, as polished as your sword. ~ Richard Sheridan

- Fencing is a game of subtlety, and bluff can be met with counter-bluff. ~ Charles L. de Beaumont

- The sword conquered for a while, but the spirit conquers for ever! ~ Sholem Asch

- Why, then the world's mine oyster; which I with sword will open. ~ Shakespeare

- The essence of fencing is to give, but by no means to receive. ~ Molière

- Never give a sword to a man who can't dance. ~ Confucius

- And each man stands with his face in the light of his own drawn sword, ready to do what a hero can. ~ Elizabeth Barrett Browning

- It's not the length of the blade, it's how you use it.

- Hold your sword as if you were holding a bird in your hand: not too lightly to prevent his escape and not too tightly to prevent him choking. ~ Justin Lafauger

- Fencing: It's all fun and games till someone loses an eye.

Figure & Speed Skating

- Blade Runner
- Figure This Figure Eight
- Free Style
- Gliding Light
- Go Figure
- Hitting the Ice
- Ice Ace
- Ice Age
- Ice Angel
- Ice Fairies
- Ice, Ice, Baby!
- Ice Princess
- Ice Sculptures
- Icing on the Season
- Just a Skater Boy/Girl

- Kiss My Ice!
- Michelle Kwan /Scott Hamilton Wanna-Be
- No, Zamboni is Not a Pasta
- On One Blade
- On the Edge with Todd Eldredge
- Peggy Fleming/Brian Boitano, Eat Your Heart Out
- A Perfect Figure Eight
- Sit Spin
- Sk8er
- Skating Through Life
- Slippin' and Slidin'
- Smooth as Glass
- Smooth as Ice
- Spinning Like a Top
- The Hardest Part of Skating is the Ice
- Watch Out! I Haven't Learned to Stop!
- Well Flutz!
- If you can't dazzle them with your performance, then blind them with your sequins.
- If figure skating was easy, it would be called hockey.
- Figure skating is a mixture of art and sport. ~ Katarina Witt
- Skating was the vessel into which I could pour my heart and soul. ~ Peggy Fleming
- Pain is short lived, but pride lasts a lifetime. ~ Elvis Stojko
- Remember: When they make the ice, they make it slippery side up. ~ Dewy Browning
- In skating over thin ice our safety is our speed. ~ Ralph Waldo Emerson
- What was really funny is that as I got older all those guys who called me a sissy in junior high school wanted me to be their best friend because they wanted to meet all the girls that I knew in figure skating. ~ Scott Hamilton
- I don't remember the first time I skated on ice, I was too young. I do remember falling in love with that wind-in-my-face feeling while speed skating. ~ Bonnie Blair
- Giving life to music through skating was something I wanted to be known for. ~ Peggy Fleming
- And the fact that I liked to show off and be the center of attention really lends itself to figure skating very well. ~ Scott Hamilton

89

- I didn't lose the gold, I won the silver. ~ Michelle Kwan

- If you think figure skating isn't a sport, try doing a scratch spin at over 250 rpm.

- The worst thing is to be paralyzed by fear. It's better to fall trying. Then you learn what to do so you don't fall again. ~ Brian Boitano

Fishing

- All I Need to Know from Life I Learned from Fishing

- Angler's Heaven

- "Carpe Diem" Does Not Mean "Fish of the Day"

- Bait Sold Here

- The Best Things in Life... are Fish

- The "Big One" Got Away

- Born to Fish, Forced to Work!

- Carpe Diem: Seize the Fish

- Cast Everything in the Best Possible Light!

- Casting 101

- The Catch of the Day

- Cattails and Cottonwoods

- Caught Our Limit

- Caution: There's Something Fishy about This Fella

- Down at the Ol' Fishin' Hole

- Down by the Riverside

- The Early Cat Gets the Fish

- The Early Worm Catches the Fish

- Fish and You Will Receive!

- Fish Come to Those Who Bait

- Fish for Dinner

- Fish More... Work Less

- Fish On!

- Fish or Cut Bait

- Fish Stories Told Here... Some True!

- A Fish Story He Never Tells...

- Fish Tales Told Here...

- Fish Tremble at the Sound of My Name

- Fisherman and Other Liars Welcome!

- Fisherman's Delight

- Fishermen Fall For It; Hook, Line and Sinker

- Fishing for Compliments

- Fishing from Dawn to Dusk

- Fishing Fun

- Fishing is Easy... Catching is Hard

- Fishing is the Sport of Drowning Worms

- Get Reel! Go Fishing!
- Get Your Bass in Gear!
- Go Fish
- Gone Fishin'
- Gone Fishin'... be Back at Dark-thirty!
- Gone Fishin'... be Back Someday!
- Good Things Come to Those Who Bait
- Good Things Come to Those Who Wade
- Here Fishy, Fishy, Fishy!
- Hook, Line and Sinker!
- Hooked on Fishing
- Hooked!
- I Came, I Saw, I Fished
- I Caught a Fish... This Big
- I Don't Exaggerate... I Just Remember Big!
- I Fish... Therefore I am
- I Never Met a Fish I Didn't Like
- I Only Fish on Days That End in "Y"
- If The Hat Is Missin'... I've Gone Fishin'
- If Wishes were Fishes, We'd Have a Fish Fry
- I'm Hooked on Fishing
- I'm on a Fishin' Mission
- It Takes Two to Tangle
- Let's Go Fishing
- Life is for the Fishing!
- The Livin' is Easy
- Make Fishin' Your Mission!
- May All Your Fishes Come True
- My Dad's a Reel Catch
- My Wish: To Catch a Fat Fish
- Never Fish and Tell
- Nice Bass!
- One Good Catch Deserves Another
- A Reel Expert Can Tackle Anything
- Reel Men Tie Their Own Flies
- Rod and Reel
- Sitting on the Dock of the Bay
- Shut Up and Fish!
- Something's Fishy
- Spare the Rod, Spoil the Day!
- Take Time to Smell the Fish
- Tall Fish Tales Told Here
- TGIF—Thank God I Fish
- There are Bigger Fish to Fry!
- This Too Shall Cast

- Wading is the Hardest Part
- Walk Tall and Carry a Big Fish!
- Water You Doing?
- Welcome Fishermen; Landlubbers by Appointment!
- What a Catch!
- When in Doubt, Exaggerate!
- Wishin' I'd Gone Fishin'...
- You Catch 'Em, You Clean 'Em
- You Should Have Seen the One That Got Away
- Of all the liars among mankind, the fisherman is the most trustworthy.
  ~ William Sherwood Fox
- Till fish do us part!
  ~ Beatrice Cook
- The fishing was good; it was the catching that was bad.
  ~ A.K. Best
- Old fisherman never die, they just smell that way!
- A woman who has never seen her husband fishing, doesn't know what a patient man she married!
- Trout that doesn't think two jumps and several runs ahead of the average fisherman is mighty apt to get fried. ~ Beatrice Cook
- The four Bs of fishing: boat, bait, beer, and BS.

- Reading about baseball is a lot more interesting than reading about chess, but you have to wonder: don't any of these guys ever go fishing? ~ Dave Shiflett
- Fishing isn't a matter of life and death... it's much more important than that.
- Scholars have long known that fishing eventually turns men into philosophers. Unfortunately, it is almost impossible to buy decent tackle on a philosopher's salary. ~ Patrick F. McManus
- A bad day of fishing is still better than a good day at the office!
- A fisherman is a jerk on one end of the line waiting for a jerk on the other.
- All fishermen are liars; it's an occupational disease with them like housemaid's knee or editor's ulcers. ~ Beatrice Cook
- All the romance of trout fishing exists in the mind of the angler and is in no way shared by the fish.
  ~ Harold F. Blaisdell
- There are two types of fisherman: those who fish for sport and those who fish for fish. ~ Unknown

- An old fisherman lives here... with the catch of his life.

- This planet is covered with sordid men who demand that he who spends time fishing shall show returns in fish. ~ Leonidas Hubbard, Jr.

- Fisherman's prayer: Lord help me to catch a fish so large that, even in the tell of it, I never need to lie.

- Bragging may not bring happiness, but no man having caught a large fish goes home through an alley. ~ Unknown

- Enjoy thy stream, o harmless fish; and when an angler for his dish, through gluttony's vile sin, attempts, the wretch, to pull thee out, God give thee strength, o gentle trout, to pull the rascal in! ~ John Wolcot

- Calling fishing a hobby is like calling brain surgery a job.
  ~ Paul Schullery

- Even eminent chartered accountants are known, in their capacity as fishermen, blissfully to ignore differences between seven and ten inches, half a pound and two pounds, three fish and a dozen fish.
  ~ William Sherwood Fox

- Even if you've been fishing for three hours and haven't gotten anything except poison ivy and sunburn, you're still better off than the worm. ~ Unknown

- Even the best lines get weak after they have been used a few times.

- Fish: an animal that grows the fastest between the time it's caught and the time the fisherman describes it to his friends.

- Early to bed. Early to rise. Fish all day. Tell big lies.

- One fish, two fish, red fish, blue fish. ~ Dr. Seuss

- Somebody just back of you while you are fishing is as bad as someone looking over your shoulder while you write a letter to your girl. ~ Ernest Hemingway

- Even a fish wouldn't get into trouble if he kept his mouth shut.

- Fishing is a discipline in the equality of men—for all men are equal before fish.
  ~ Herbert Hoover

- Fishing is boring, unless you catch an actual fish, and then it is disgusting.
  ~ Dave Barry

- I fish better with a lit cigar; some people fish better with talent. ~ Nick Lyons

- There he stands, draped in more equipment than a telephone lineman, trying to outwit an organism with a brain no bigger than a breadcrumb and getting licked in the process.
  ~ Paul O'Neil

- The bass are always bigger on the other side of the boat.

- Fishing is much more than fish. It is the great occasion when we may return to the fine simplicity of our forefathers. ~ Herbert Hoover

- Fishy, fishy in the brook, papa catch him on a hook, mama fry him in a pan, baby eat him like a man.
  ~ Children's song

- Give a man a fish and feed him for a day... teach a man to fish and get rid of him for a weekend.
  ~ Zenna Schaffer

- If you've got short, stubby fingers and wear reading glasses, any relaxation you would normally derive from fly fishing is completely eliminated when you try to tie on a fly. ~ Jack Ohman

- Give a man a fish, and he can eat for a day. But teach a man how to fish, and he'll be dead of mercury poisoning inside of three years. ~ Charles Haas

- I am not against golf, since I cannot but suspect it keeps armies of the unworthy from discovering trout. ~ Paul O'Neil

- If people concentrated on the really important things in life, there'd be a shortage of fishing poles.
  ~ Doug Larson

- Fishing tournaments seem a little like playing tennis with living balls. ~ Jim Harrison

- It has always been my private conviction that any man who pits his intelligence against a fish and loses has it coming. ~ John Steinbeck

- Many men go fishing all of their lives without knowing that it is not fish they are after. ~ Thoreau

- May the holes in your net be no larger than the fish in it.
  ~ Irish Blessing

- My biggest worry is that my wife (when I'm dead) will sell my fishing gear for what I said I paid for it.
  ~ Koos Brandt

- Nothing makes a fish bigger than almost being caught. ~ Unknown

- Our tradition is that of the first man who sneaked away to the creek when the tribe did not really need fish. ~ Roderick Haig-Brown

- There is no such thing as too much equipment.

- To fish is human, to throw back is divine.

- People who fish for food, and sport be damned, are called pot-fishermen. The more expert ones are called crack pot-fishermen. All other fishermen are called crackpot fishermen. This is confusing. ~ Ed Zern

- There is certainly something in angling that tends to produce a serenity of the mind. ~ Washington Irving

- The gods do not deduct from man's allotted span the hours spent in fishing. ~ Babylonian Proverb

- Sometimes you really have to squirm to get off the hook.

- The charm of fishing is that it is the pursuit of what is elusive but attainable, a perpetual series of occasions for hope. ~ John Buchan

- Men and fish are alike—they both get into trouble when they open their mouths.

- The fishing is always better on the other side of the lake.

- Never open a can of worms unless you plan on fishing.

- There is no greater fan of fly fishing than the worm. ~ Patrick F. McManus

- Vegetarian is an old Indian word for "bad fisherman."

- There will be days when the fishing is better than one's most optimistic forecast, others when it is far worse. Either is a gain over just staying home. ~ Roderick Haig-Brown

- There's a fine line between fishing and just standing on the shore like an idiot. ~ Steven Wright

- Fish, to taste good, must swim three times: in water, in butter, and in wine. ~ Proverb

- Three-fourths of the earth's surface is water, and one-fourth is land. It is quite clear that the good Lord intended us to spend triple the amount of time fishing as taking care of the lawn. ~ Chuck Clark

- Time's fun when you're tying flies.
- To fish or not to fish... Not to fish? Yeah... like that's even an option!
- We ask a simple question and that is all we wish: Are fishermen all liars? Or do only liars fish? ~ William Sherwood Fox
- There's no taking trout with dry breeches. ~ Miguel De Cervantes
- You must lose a fly to catch a trout. ~ George Herbert

Flying Disc

- Bad Tree!
- Disc Taco
- Dogs Love Me
- Duck!
- Flying Free
- Flying Saucers
- Give 'n' Go
- Good Dog!
- On the Roof Again
- Stupid Cross-breeze!
- UFOs
- The most powerful force in the world is that of a disc straining to get under a car.

- The only thing disc golf needs to make it perfect is a little disc golf cart.
- When a ball dreams, it dreams it's a Frisbee. ~ Stancil Johnson
- We used to say that Frisbee is really a religion— "Frisbeeterians," we'd call ourselves. When we die, we don't go to purgatory, we just land up on the roof and lie there. ~ Ed Headrick
- The greatest single aid to distance is for the disc to be going in a direction you did not want. ~ Dan Roddick
- Sometimes I wonder, "Why is that Frisbee getting bigger?" And then it hits me. ~ T-shirt

Football

- And It's Good!
- Are You Ready for Some Football?
- Backfield in Motion
- Backyard Football
- Conference Championship
- Defense or Offense
- Defensive Line or Offensive Line
- Double Days [high school practices]

SNAPPY SNIPPETS THAT SCORE!

- Fall Preview
- First and Ten
- First Down
- Flag Football
- Football Banquet
- Football Fan
- Football Fever
- Football Fun
- Football is a Kick
- Football Players Will Tackle Anything!
- Football Star
- Football—Not Just a Game
- Fumble
- Give Me the Pig Skin
- Go the Whole Nine Yards
- Go for Two!
- Go! Fight! Win!
- GOALS [use football for O]
- Gridiron
- Hail Mary Pass
- Half-Time
- Half-Time Entertainment
- Hang Time
- Hard Nose, Smash Mouth, Football!
- Homecoming

- Instant Replay
- It's Overtime!
- Junior Varsity
- Just for Kicks
- Kicking Off the Season
- Let's Do It Again!
- The Monday Morning Quarterbacks
- My Touchdown Dance
- On Any Given Sunday
- On the Bench—Picking up Slivers
- Oops! That Had to Hurt!
- Penalty!
- Powder-puff
- Quarterback Sneak
- Super Bowl, Here We Come
- Super Bowl Party
- The Longest Yard
- They Put on Their Pads... They Pay the Price!
- This is Touch Football?
- Three Minute Warning
- Time to Tackle Another Year
- Touchdown!
- Two-a-Days
- Unnecessary Roughness!
- Varsity

- Water Boy/Girl
- Weekend Quarterback
- What's Soccer?
- You Gotta be a Football Hero
- Football is like life, it requires perseverance, self denial, hard work, sacrifice, dedication and respect for authority. ~ Vince Lombardi
- If God wanted football played in the spring, he would not have invented baseball. ~ Sam Rutigliano
- A school without football is in danger of deteriorating into a medieval study hall. ~ Vince Lombardi
- Academe, n.: an ancient school where morality and philosophy were taught. Academy, n.: [from academe] a modern school where football is taught. ~ Ambrose Bierce
- At the base of it was the urge, if you wanted to play football, to knock someone down, that was what the sport was all about, the will to win closely linked with contact. ~ George Plimpton
- Fans never fall asleep at our games because they're afraid they might get hit by a pass. ~ George Raveling

- College football is a sport that bears the same relation to education that bullfighting does to agriculture. ~ Elbert Hubbard
- Football is, after all, a wonderful way to get rid of your aggressions without going to jail for it. ~ Heywood Hale Brown
- Football is a mistake. It combines the two worst elements of American life. It is violence punctuated by committee meetings. ~ George Will
- Football is a very short-term proposition. Football really prepares you for nothing. The only thing I got out of football was the ability to work hard, and that's it. ~ Gale Sayers
- Football is like life—it requires perseverance, self -denial, hard work, sacrifice, dedication and respect for authority. ~ Vince Lombardi
- Football is not a game, but a religion, a metaphysical island of fundamental truth in a highly verbalized, disguised society, a throwback of 30,000 generations of anthropological time. ~ Arnold Mandell

- Baseball is what we were. Football is what we have become. ~ Mary Mcgrory

- Australian Rules football might best be described as a game devised for padded cells, played in the open air. ~ Jim Murray

- Football isn't a contact sport, it's a collision sport. Dancing is a contact sport. ~ Vince Lombardi and Duffy Daugherty

- Football players, like prostitutes, are in the business of ruining their bodies for the pleasure of strangers. ~ Merle Kessler

- American football makes rugby look like a Tupperware party. ~ Sue Lawley,

- For me, winning isn't something that happens suddenly on the field when the whistle blows and the crowds roar. Winning is something that builds physically and mentally every day that you train and every night that you dream. ~ Emmitt Smith

- The reason women don't play football is because eleven of them would never wear the same outfit in public. ~ Phyllis Diller

- He treats us like men. He lets us wear earrings. ~ Torrin Polk, on Coach Jenkins

- Gentlemen, it is better to have died as a small boy than to fumble this football. ~ John Heisman

- He was the only man I ever saw who ran his own interference. ~ Steve Owen, on Bronko Nagurski

- When it comes to football, God is prejudiced—toward big, fast kids. ~ Chuck Mills

- I do not like football, which I think of as a game in which two tractors approach each other from opposite directions and collide. Besides, I have contempt for a game in which players have to wear so much equipment. Men play basketball in their underwear, which seems just right to me. ~ Anna Quindlen

- Rugby is a beastly game played by gentlemen. Soccer is a gentleman's game played by beasts. Football is a beastly game played by beasts. ~ Henry Blaha

- I'm not allowed to comment on lousy referees. ~ Jim Finks, on what he thought of the officials' decisions

- We didn't lose the game; we just ran out of time. ~ Vince Lombardi

- Maybe a good rule in life is never become too important to do your own laundry. ~ Barry Sanders

- Men are clinging to football on a level we aren't even aware of. For centuries, we ruled everything, and now, in the last ten minutes, there are all these incursions by women. It's our Alamo. ~ Tony Kornheiser

- I have seen women walk right past a TV set with a football game on and—this always amazes me—not stop to watch, even if the TV is showing replays of what we call a 'good hit', which is a tackle that causes at least one major internal organ to actually fly out of a player's body. ~ Dave Barry

- I wouldn't ever set out to hurt anyone deliberately unless it was, you know, important—like a league game or something. ~ Dick Butkus

- Most football players are temperamental. That's 90 percent temper and 10 percent mental. ~ Doug Plank

- The Rose Bowl is the only bowl I've ever seen that I didn't have to clean. ~ Erma Bombeck

- In short, in life, as in a football game, the principle to follow is: hit the line hard; don't foul and don't shirk, but hit the line hard! ~ Theodore Roosevelt

- Let's face it, you have to have a slightly recessive gene that has a little something to do with the brain to go out on the football field and beat your head against other human beings on a daily basis. ~ Tim Green

- One of the great disappointments of a football game is that the cheerleaders never seem to get injured. ~ Unknown

- Pro football is like nuclear warfare. There are no winners, only survivors. ~ Frank Gifford

- Some people think football is a matter of life and death. I assure you, it's much more serious than that. ~ Bill Shankly

- Speed, strength and the inability to register pain immediately. ~ Reggie Williams, on his greatest strengths as a football player

- Sure, luck means a lot in football. Not having a good quarterback is bad luck. ~ Don Schula

- If winning isn't everything, why do they keep score? ~ Vince Lombardi

- Thanksgiving dinners take eighteen hours to prepare. They are consumed in twelve minutes. Half—times take twelve minutes. This is not coincidence. ~ Erma Bombeck

- I've been big ever since I was little.
  ~ William "The Refrigerator" Perry

- We interrupt this marriage to bring you football season.

- If you don't want to get tackled, don't carry the ball. ~ Ann McKay Thompson

- If you're mad at your kid, you can either raise him to be a nose tackle or send him out to play on the freeway. It's about the same. ~ Bob Golic

- The pads don't keep you from getting hurt. They just keep you from getting killed. ~ Chad Bratzke

- I like to believe that my best hits border on felonious assault.
  ~ Jack Tatum

- There are several differences between a football game and a revolution. For one thing, a football game usually lasts longer and the participants wear uniforms. Also, there are usually more casualties in a football game. The object of the game is to move a ball past the other team's goal line. This counts as six points. No points are given for lacerations, contusions, or abrasions—but then no points are deducted, either. Kicking is very important in football. In fact, some of the more enthusiastic players even kick the ball, occasionally.
  ~ Alfred Hitchcock

- Sectional football games have the glory and the despair of war...
  ~ John Steinbeck

- If a man watches three football games in a row, he should be declared legally dead. ~ Erma Bombeck

- Football is an incredible game. Sometimes it's so incredible, it's unbelievable.
  ~ Tom Landry

- You have to play this game like somebody just hit your mother with a two-by-four. ~ Dan Birdwell

- Trying to maintain order during a legalized gang brawl involving 80 toughs with a little whistle, a hanky and a ton of prayer.
  ~ Anonymous referee, on his job

- I would love to play football; who wouldn't want to tackle those boys!

- What about football? Is it a sport or a concussion?
  ~ Jim Murray

- What's the worst thing that can happen to a quarterback? He loses his confidence. ~ Terry Bradshaw

- It was an ideal day for football—too cold for the spectators and too cold for the players. ~ Red Smith

- When I went to Catholic high school in Philadelphia, we just had one coach for football and basketball. He took all of us who turned out and had us run through a forest. The ones who ran into the trees were on the football team. ~ George Raveling

- Winning is a habit, unfortunately so is losing.
  ~ Vince Lombardi

- There is only one way to succeed in anything and that is to give it everything.
  ~ Vince Lombardi

Golf

- Absolutely Divot-ing!
- Another Ball in the Trees
- Any Time is Tee Time
- Big Shot
- Born to Golf, Forced to Work
- Bye-Bye, Birdie
- Caddy Shack
- Calling the Shots
- Cheap Shot
- Chip Shot
- Daddy's Caddy
- Designated Driver
- Diamond in the Rough
- Double Bogey
- Drivin' Around
- Drivin' My Life Away
- Eat... Sleep... Golf
- A Few Irons in the Fire
- Fore-Ever Golfing
- Fore! OK, Maybe 3 1/2?
- Future Tiger Woods
- Golf [use a ball for the O]
- Golf is 95% Mental Anguish
- Golf Lessons
- Golf Suits Me to a Tee

- Golf—It's Not Just a Game
- The Golfer's Diet: Stay on the Greens
- The Grass is Always Greener... Around the Hole
- The Greatest Golfers: Palmer, Player, Nicklaus, Watson, Kite, Trevino, Woods, and _____
- Green with Envy
- Grip It and Rip It
- Hazards Attract and Fairways Repel
- Hunting for Birdies
- I Only Golf on Days That End with "Y"
- If the Hat Can't be Seen... I'm on the Green!
- If There is No Golf in Heaven... I'm Not Going!
- I'm Happy when I'm Teed Off
- I'm Not over the Hill, I'm on the Back Nine
- In Full Swing
- Iron Fist
- Iron Man
- It Went Where?
- Just Puttering Around
- The Masters—Here I Come
- On the Green
- On the Green in Two
- Par Excellence
- A Parting Shot
- Playing Through
- Square Ball in a Round Hole
- Tee and Sympathy
- Tee for Two
- Tee Party
- Tee Time
- Tee'd Off
- Teeing Off
- Now for the Tee-Off
- Thank Your Lucky Stars
- There's No Time like Tee Time
- Tiger Woods Wanna-be
- To Golf or Not to Golf? What a Silly Question!
- When's Tee Time?
- You "Putt" Me in a Great Mood
- You Can Never Start Too Young!
- If you watch a game, it's fun. If you play it, it's recreation. If you work at it, it's golf. ~ Bob Hope
- Golf is a day spent in a round of strenuous idleness. ~ William Wordsworth

- Golf, like measles, should be caught young. ~ P.G. Wodehouse

- I'd give up golf if I didn't have so many sweaters. ~ Bob Hope

- "After all, golf is only a game," said Millicent. Women say these things without thinking. It does not mean that there is a kink in their character. They simply don't realize what they are saying. ~ P.G. Wodehouse

- Faith has its share of bunkers, and golf has its share of prayers. ~ Max Lucado

- Golf is a good walk spoiled. ~ Mark Twain

- Golf is deceptively simple and endlessly complicated. It satisfies the soul and frustrates the intellect. It is at the same time rewarding and maddening—it is without a doubt the greatest game mankind has ever invented. ~ Arnold Palmer

- Golf is good for the soul. You get so mad at yourself you forget to hate your enemies. ~ Will Rogers

- A "gimme" can best be defined as an agreement between two golfers, neither of whom can putt very well. ~ Unknown

- "Play it as it lies" is one of the fundamental dictates of golf. The other is "wear it if it clashes." ~ Henry Beard

- A bad day at the golf course still beats a good day at the office.

- Show me a man who is a good loser and I'll show you a man who is playing golf with his boss. ~ Unknown

- There are two things you can do with your head down, play golf and pray. ~ Lee Trevino

- Golf is like chasing a quinine pill around a cow pasture. ~ Winston Churchill

- My swing is so bad I look like a caveman killing his lunch. ~ Lee Trevino

- Nothing dissects a man in public quite like golf. ~ Brent Musberger

- A ball you can see in the rough from 50 yards away is not yours.

- Give me the fresh air, a beautiful partner and a nice round of golf, and you can keep the fresh air and the round of golf. ~ Jack Benny

- They call it golf because all the other four letter words are taken.

- These greens are so fast I have to hold my putter over the ball and hit it with the shadow. ~ Sam Snead

- A game in which you claim the privileges of age and retain the play-things of childhood. ~ Unknown

- They say golf is like life, but don't believe them. Golf is more complicated than that. ~ Gardner Dickinson

- A golf ball is like a clock. Always hit it at 6 o'clock and make it go toward 12 o'clock. But make sure you're in the same time zone. ~ Chi Chi Rodriguez

- No game designed to be played with the aid of personal servants by right-handed men who can't even bring along their dogs can be entirely good for the soul. ~ Bruce Mccall

- A hole-in-one is amazing when you think of the different universes this white mass of molecules has to pass through on its way to the hole. ~ Mac O'Grady

- A passion, an obsession, a romance, a nice acquaintanceship with trees, sand and water. ~ Bob Ryan

- Give me life, liberty and the pursuit of golf balls.

- Actually, the only time I ever took out a one-iron was to kill a tarantula. And it took a seven to do that. ~ Jim Murray

- After all these years, it's still embarrassing for me to play on the American golf tour. Like the time I asked my caddie for a sand wedge and he came back ten minutes later with a ham on rye. ~ Chi Chi Rodriguez, on his accent

- All I've got against it is that it takes you so far from the clubhouse. ~ Eric Linklater

- Counting on your opponent to inform you when he breaks a rule is like expecting him to make fun of his own haircut.

- His driving is unbelievable. I don't go that far on my holidays. ~ Ian Baker-Finch, on John Daly

- Forget your opponents; always play against par. ~ Sam Snead

- I brought an extra pair of pants today, thought I'd might get a hole in one!

- Don't drink and drive... you might slice a hook.

- Although golf was originally restricted to wealthy Protestants, today it's open to anybody who owns hideous clothing. ~ Dave Barry

- Don't play too much golf. Two rounds a day are plenty. ~ Harry Vardon

- Any game where a man 60 can beat a man 30 ain't no game. ~ Burt Shotten

- Art said he wanted to get more distance. I told him to hit it and run backward.
  ~ Ken Venturi, on Art Rosenbaum

- Baseball players quit playing and they take up golf. Basketball players quit, take up golf. Football players quit, take up golf. What are we supposed to take up when we quit?
  ~ George Archer

- But you don't have to go up in the stands and play your foul balls. I do.
  ~ Sam Snead, to Ted Williams, on baseball vs. golf

- Columbus went around the world in 1492. That isn't a lot of strokes when you consider the course.
  ~ Lee Trevino

- Golf is a game in which you yell "fore," shoot six, and write down five.

- Drugs are very much a part of professional sports today, but when you think about it, golf is the only sport where the players aren't penalized for being on grass.
  ~ Bob Hope

- Golf appeals to the idiot in us and the child. Just how childlike golf players become is proven by their frequent inability to count past five. ~ John Updike

- Eighteen holes of match or medal play will teach you more about your foe than will 18 years of dealing with him across a desk.
  ~ Grantland Rice

- Golf is a game that is played on a five-inch course—the distance between your ears.
  ~ Bobby Jones

- Even God has to practice his putting. ~ Golf Saying

- Every time a golfer makes a birdie, he must subsequently make two triple bogeys to restore the fundamental equilibrium of the universe.

- Golf can best be defined as an endless series of tragedies obscured by the occasional miracle. ~ Unknown

- Find a man with both feet firmly on the ground and you've found a man about to make a difficult putt.
  ~ Fletcher Knebel

- Don't buy a putter until you've had a chance to throw it.

- Golf balls are attracted to water as unerringly as the eye of a middle-aged man to a female bosom.
  ~ Michael Green

- Fifty years ago, 100 white men chasing one black man across a field was called the Ku Klux Klan. Today it's called the PGA tour.
  ~ Unknown, on Tiger Woods

- Yeah, after each of my downhill putts.
  ~ Homero Blancas, asked if he had any uphill putts

- Golf is a day spent in a round of strenuous idleness. ~ William Wordsworth

- You are meant to play the ball as it lies, a fact that may help to touch on your own objective approach to life. ~ Grantland Rice

- Golf combines two favorite American pastimes: taking long walks and hitting things with a stick. ~ P.J. O'Rourke

- Golf gives you an insight into human nature, your own as well as your opponent's. ~ Grantland Rice

- Golf is a fascinating game. It has taken me nearly forty years to discover that I can't play it. ~ Ted Ray

- Duffers who consistently shank their balls are urged to buy and study Shanks—No Thanks by R.K. Hoffman, or in extreme cases, M.S. Howard's excellent Tennis for Beginners. ~ Henry Beard

- Golf is a game in which the ball lies poorly and the players well. ~ Art Rosenbaum

- One thing about golf is you don't know why you play bad and why you play good.
  ~ George Archer

- If I hit it right, it's a slice. If I hit it left, it's a hook. If I hit it straight, it's a miracle. ~ Unknown

- He who has the fastest cart... never has a bad lie.

- If I'm on the course and lightning starts, I get inside fast. If God wants to play through, let him. ~ Bob Hope

- Golf is a game that was invented to punish those who retire early.

- Golf is an awkward set of bodily contortions designed to produce a graceful result.
  ~ Tommy Armour

- One under a tree, one under a bush, one under the water.
  ~ Lee Trevino, on how he was one under during a tournament

- Golf is a lot of walking, broken up by disappointment and bad arithmetic.

- Real golfers don't cry when they line up their fourth putt.

- Golf is a steady diet of greens.

- If you really want to get better at golf, go back and take it up at a much earlier age.

- Golf is an ineffectual attempt to put an elusive ball into an obscure hole with implements ill-adapted to the purpose.
  ~ Woodrow Wilson

- If you think it's hard to meet new people, try picking up the wrong golf ball. ~ Jack Lemmon

- Golf is an open exhibition of overweening ambition, courage deflated by stupidity, skill scoured by a whiff of arrogance.
  ~ Alistair Cooke

- Golf is essentially an exercise in masochism conducted out-of-doors.
  ~ Paul O'Neil

- Heaven seems a little closer when your house is near the golf course.

- Golf is golf. You hit the ball, you go find it. Then you hit it again. ~ Lon Hinkle

- I golf because the doctor told me to take "iron" everyday.

- Golf is life. If you can't take golf, you can't take life. ~ Unknown

- Real golfers, no matter what the provocation, never strike a caddie with the driver. The sand wedge is far more effective.
  ~ Huxtable Pippey

- Golf is not just an exercise; it's an adventure, a romance, a Shakespeare play in which disaster and comedy are intertwined.
  ~ Harold Segall

- I don't know how I can play so well and score so bad.

- Golf is not, on the whole, a game for realists. By its exactitudes of measurements it invites the attention of perfectionists.
  ~ Heywood Hale Broun

- Golf is an easy game... it's just hard to play

- One of the most fascinating things about golf is how it reflects the cycle of life. No matter what you shoot—the next day you have to go back to the first tee and begin all over again and make yourself into something. ~ Peter Jacobsen

- Golf is the cruelest game, because eventually it will drag you out in front of the whole school, take your lunch money and slap you around. ~ Rick Reilly

- If there is any larceny in a man, golf will bring it out. ~ Paul Gallico

- Golf is hockey at the halt. ~ Arthur Marshall

- The reason the pro tells you to keep your head down is so you can't see him laughing. ~ Phyllis Diller

- Golf isn't like other sports where you can take a player out if he's having a bad day. You have to play the whole game. ~ Phil Blackmar

- If a lot of people gripped a knife and fork the way they do a golf club, they'd starve to death. ~ Sam Snead

- Gone golfin'... be back at dark thirty. ~ Unknown

- If there is a ball in the fringe and a ball in the bunker, your ball is in the bunker. If both balls are in the bunker, yours is in the footprint.

- Have you ever noticed what golf spells backwards? ~ Al Boliska

- I'd play every day if I could. It's cheaper than a shrink and there are no telephones on my golf cart. ~ Brent Musburger

- The average golfer doesn't play golf. He attacks it. ~ Jack Burke

- I can airmail the golf ball, but sometimes I don't put the right address on it. ~ Jim Dent

- I don't like watching golf on TV. I can't stand whispering. ~ David Brenner

- I just hope I don't have to explain all the times I've used his name in vain when I get up there. ~ Bob Hope

- Golfer's prayer: Lord may I live long enough to shoot my age.

- If you break 100, watch your golf. If you break 80, watch your business. ~ Joey Adams

- If only I could swing like I do in practice.

- The least thing upset him on the links. He missed short putts because of the uproar of butterflies in the adjoining meadows. ~ P.G. Wodehouse

- I guess there is nothing that will get your mind off everything like golf. I have never been depressed enough to take up the game, but they say you get so sore at yourself you forget to hate your enemies. ~ Will Rogers

- The best wood in most amateurs' bags is the pencil. ~ Unknown

- I hate golf, I hate golf, I hate golf... Nice shot! I love golf.

- Golf: I'd quit the stupid game if I wasn't married.

- I have a tip that can take five strokes off anyone's golf game: it's called an eraser. ~ Arnold Palmer

- The income tax has made more liars out of the American people than golf has. ~ Will Rogers

- I know I am getting better at golf because I'm hitting fewer spectators. ~ Gerald Ford

- May thy ball lie in green pastures and not in still waters. ~ Unknown

- Some of us worship in churches, some in synagogues, some on golf courses. ~ Adlai Stevenson

- If I can hit a curveball, why can't I hit a ball that is standing still on a course? ~ Larry Nelson

- Swinging at daisies is like playing electric guitar with a tennis racket; if it were that easy, we could all be Jerry Garcia. The ball changes everything. ~ Michael Bamberger

- If you drink, don't drive. Don't even putt. ~ Dean Martin

- My doctor says to live on greens.

- I never pray to God to make a putt. I pray to God to help me react good if I miss a putt. ~ Chi Chi Rodriguez

- My handicap? Woods and irons. ~ Chris Codiroli

- I play in the low 80s. If it's any hotter than that, I won't play. ~ Joe E. Lewis

- The ardent golfer would play Mount Everest if somebody put a flagstick on top. ~ Pete Dye

- I regard golf as an expensive way of playing marbles. ~ G.K. Chesterton

- Talking to a golf ball won't do you any good. Unless you do it while your opponent is teeing off. ~ Bruce Lansky

- I would like to deny all allegations by Bob Hope that during my last game of golf, I hit an eagle, a birdie, an elk and a moose. ~ Gerald Ford

- If frustration and humiliation is your aim, then golf is your game.

- The shortest distance between any two points on a golf course is a straight line that passes directly through the center of a very large tree.

- Reverse every natural instinct and do the opposite of what you are inclined to do, and you will probably come very close to having a perfect golf swing. ~ Ben Hogan

- If profanity had an influence on the flight of the ball, the game of golf would be played far better than it is. ~ Horace G. Hutchinson

- Golf, like the measles, should be caught young, for, if postponed to riper years, the results may be serious. ~ P.G. Wodehouse

- Playing the game I have learned the meaning of humility. It has given me an understanding of futility of the human effort. ~ Abba Eban

- My body is here, but my mind has already teed off.

- I'm hitting the woods just great, but I'm having a terrible time getting out of them. ~ Harry Toscano

- Golf is played by twenty million mature American men whose wives think they are out having fun. ~ Jim Bishop

- If you wish to hide your character, do not play golf. ~ Percey Boomer

- The golf swing is like a suitcase into which we are trying to pack one too many things. ~ John Updike

- Golf is like a love affair. If you don't take it seriously, it's no fun; if you do take it seriously, it breaks your heart. ~ Arthur Daley

- Old golfers never die they just putter around.

- The holes are numbered.
  ~ Jack Nicklaus, when asked his secret to knowing his way around the golf course

- I'm not saying my golf game went bad, but if I grew tomatoes, they'd come up sliced.
  ~ Attributed to both Miller Barber and Lee Trevino

- If you call on God to improve the results of a shot while it is still in motion, you are using "an outside agency" and subject to appropriate penalties under the rules of golf. ~ Henry Longhurst

- Isn't it fun to go out on the course and lie in the sun? ~ Bob Hope

- Golf is not a game, it's bondage. It was obviously devised by a man torn with guilt, eager to atone for his sins. ~ Jim Murray

- I'll shoot my age if I have to live to be 105. ~ Bob Hope

- There are two kinds of bounces: unfair bounces and bounces that are just the way you meant to play them.

- Man blames fate for other accidents but feels personally responsible for a hole in one. ~ Martha Beckman

- In baseball you hit your home run over the right-field fence, the left-field fence, the center-field fence. Nobody cares. In golf everything has got to be right over second base.
  ~ Ken Harrelson

- If you want to take long walks, take long walks. If you want to hit things with sticks, hit things with sticks. But there's no excuse for combining the two and putting the results on TV. Golf is not so much a sport as an insult to lawns.
  ~ National Lampoon

- Practice puts brains in your muscles. ~ Sam Snead

- You can hit a two-acre fairway 10 percent of the time and a two-inch branch 90 percent of the time.

- If your opponent is playing several shots in vain attempts to extricate himself from a bunker, do not stand near him and audibly count his strokes. It would be justifiable homicide if he wound up his pitiable exhibition by applying his niblick to your head. ~ Harry Vardon

- The worst club in my bag is my brain. ~ Chris Perry

- Men who would face torture without a word become blasphemous at the short fourteenth. It is clear that the game of golf may well be included in that category of intolerable provocations which may legally excuse or mitigate behavior not otherwise excusable.
  ~ A.P. Herbert

- John certainly gives it a good hit, doesn't he? My Sunday best is a Wednesday afternoon compared to him.
  ~ Nick Faldo, on John Daly

- I'm a golfaholic, no question about that. Counseling wouldn't help me. They'd have to put me in prison, and then I'd talk the warden into building a hole or two and teach him how to play. ~ Lee Trevino

- If you're caught on a golf course during a storm and are afraid of lightning, hold up a 1-iron. Not even God can hit a 1-iron.
  ~ Lee Trevino

- I'm about five inches from being an outstanding golfer. That's the distance my left ear is from my right. ~ Ben Crenshaw

- It's a funny thing, the more I practice the luckier I get. ~ Arnold Palmer

- Through years of experience I have found that air offers less resistance than dirt.
  ~ Jack Nicklaus, on why he tees his ball high

- One almost expects one of the players to peer into the monitor and politely request viewers to refrain from munching so loudly on cheese and crackers while the golfers are trying to reach the greens.
  ~ Pete Alfano

- Golf is really my profession, show business just pays for the greens fees. ~ Bob Hope

- It took me seventeen years to get 3,000 hits. I did it in one afternoon on the golf course. ~ Hank Aaron

- One minute you're bleeding. The next minute you're hemorrhaging. The next minute you're painting the Mona Lisa.
  ~ Mac O'Grady, describing a typical round of golf

- Golf is so popular simply because it is the best game in the world at which to be bad. ~ A.A. Milne

- The trouble that most of us find with the modern matched sets of clubs is that they don't really seem to know any more about the game than the old ones did. ~ Robert Browning

- I've spent most of my life golfing... the rest I've just wasted.

- In golf, as in life, it's the follow-through that makes the difference.

- The only time my prayers are never answered is on the golf course. ~ Billy Graham

- It is more satisfying to be a bad player at golf. The worse you play, the better you remember the occasional good shot.
  ~ Nubar Gulbenkian

- In golf, you keep your head down and follow through. In the vice presidency, you keep your head up and follow through. It's a big difference. ~ Dan Quayle

- The less skilled the player, the more likely he is to share his ideas about the golf swing.

- One of the advantages bowling has over golf is that you seldom lose a bowling ball. ~ Don Carter

- It's good sportsmanship not to pick up lost balls while they are still rolling.
  ~ Mark Twain

- When you look up, causing an awful shot, you will always look down again at exactly the moment when you ought to start watching the ball if you ever want to see it again.

- It's so bad I could putt off a tabletop and still leave the ball halfway down the leg. ~ J.C. Snead

- It is almost impossible to remember how tragic a place this world is when one is playing golf. ~ Robert Lynd

- The difference between golf and government is that in golf you can't improve your lie. ~ George Deukmejian

- The uglier a man's legs are, the better he plays golf. It's almost a law. ~ H.G. Wells,

- There is no such thing as a natural touch. Touch is something you create by hitting millions of golf balls. ~ Lee Trevino

- Golf seems to me an arduous way to go for a walk. I prefer to take the dogs out.
  ~ Princess Anne of Great Britain

114

- There is one thing in this world that is dumber than playing golf. That is watching someone else playing golf. What do you actually get to see? Thirty-seven guys in polyester slacks squinting at the sun. Doesn't that set your blood racing? ~ Peter Andrews

- A golf course is nothing but a poolroom moved outdoors. ~ Barry Fitzgerald

- There's something intrinsically therapeutic about choosing to spend your time in a wide, open park-like setting that non-golfers can never truly understand. ~ Charles Rosin

- They throw their clubs backwards and that's wrong. You should always throw a club ahead of you so that you don't have to walk any extra distance to get it.
  ~ Tommy Bolt, about the tempers of modern players

- What's nice about our tour is you can't remember your bad shots.
  ~ Bob Bruce, on the Senior Tour

- To some golfers, the greatest handicap is the ability to add correctly.
  ~ Unknown

- The number of shots taken by an opponent who is out of sight is equal to the square root of the sum of the number of curses heard plus the number of swishes.
  ~ Michael Green

- When I die, bury me at the golf course so my husband will visit.

- You can't call it a sport. You don't run, jump. You don't shoot, you don't pass. All you have to do is buy some clothes that don't match. ~ Steve Sax

- A golf course outside a big town serves an excellent purpose in that it segregates... all the idle and idiot well-to-do.
  ~ Osbert Sitwell

- When I putt, my emotions collide like tectonic plates. It's left my memory circuits full of scars that won't heal. ~ Mac O'Grady

- When you hear someone shout "you da man," if he ain't shouting at Arnold Palmer, then it ain't da man. ~ Ron Green

- Trevino is in a league by himself. We don't even count him. We figure when you come in second, you're a winner. ~ Chi Chi Rodriguez

- A golf match is a test of your skill against your opponent's luck.

- What other people may find in poetry or art museums, I find in the flight of a good drive.
  ~ Arnold Palmer

Gymnastics

- Can't Hold a Candlestick to My Flexibility
- Cross the Bridge
- Eating Mat
- Flyaway to Victory
- Full of Flair
- I've Got Rhythm
- Jumping Through Hoops
- Lord of the Rings
- My Still Ring Circus
- Spot Me!
- Stick It
- Take the Floor
- Taming the Pommel Horse
- Tear the Competition to Ribbons
- Twist and Shout
- Raising the Bar
- Rounding Up Our Round Offs

- Balancing Act
- Falling with Style
- Floor Extraordinaire
- Giant Leap
- Got Chalk?
- Gymnastics Champions... Built by Gravity and Guts
- Gymnastics Make Me Flip
- Gymnasts are Better Balanced
- Gymnasts Defeat Gravity
- Hang Time [high bar or rings]
- Man Created Gymnastics— Women Perfected It!
- No Fear—No Gravity
- Nothing But Air
- One Giant Leap for Mankind
- Perfect Balance
- Perfect Ten
- Point Your Toes
- Riding to Victory on My Pommel Horse
- Round Off
- She Moves in Mysterious Ways
- She/He Gets a 10.0 from Me
- Sticks the Landing!
- Tuck and Roll

- Tumble
- Up in the Air
- What Goes up Must Come Down
- Zero Gravity
- Gymnastics uses every single part of your body, every little tiny muscle that you never even knew. ~ Shannon Miller
- I did gymnastics when I was growing up and to this day I can still do the splits. ~ Kristin Kreuk
- In the perfect world a person would be a mix of a ballerina, Stretch Armstrong, and a body builder. Or they could simply be a gymnast.
- When I go in to compete, whether it's gymnastics or anything else, I do my own thing. I compete with myself. ~ Shannon Miller
- If your not sore in gymnastics, then you're not practicing right.
- Everything a gymnast needs: A little chalk and a LOT of attitude.
- Gymnasts defy gravity.
- Flexible people don't get bent out of shape.
- Everyone gets scared, and everyone falls. The key is to get right back up and try again. ~ Shannon Miller
- In gymnastics, it is not how good you are when you started, it's how good you are when you're finished.
- One time a French reporter asked me how I could do a cross so easily. I said, "You just lower your body down until your arms are straight out to the sides, then you stop." ~ Albert Azaryan
- A shiny new leotard... $80. A new pair of grips... $40. A perfect 10 performance... priceless.
- Whenever I feel lost or I need to get my focus back I remind myself of the three Ds: determination, dedication and dynamics. They always get me back on track. ~ Dominique Dawes
- To try a laid out full, when you can't even do a tuck? No it isn't impossible, you just need a little luck.
- To be as good as Mary Lou, and win the all-around; you must be willing to get black and blue, and wait patiently to be crowned.

- Gymnastics is a vertical expression of a horizontal desire.
- After one hour of playing football, the gymnast will be bruised. After one hour of gymnastics, the football player will be dead.
- For all you cheerleaders who think you're cool, just remember... gymnasts rule!
- He/she flies through the air with the greatest of ease.
- Talent alone is not enough. I believe that a really good gymnast is 10% inspiration and 90% perspiration.
  ~ Vladislav Rastorotsky
- To be a gymnast, you need more than flexibility! You need to be an enthusiast to try an impossibility.
- Don't let anyone take your dreams away from you. Never stop short of your goal. ~ Aimee Walker
- To be as good as Nadia, and score a perfect 10; the crowd and judges you must awe, but if you fall, get up again.
- You can take the gymnast out of gymnastics but you can't take the gymnastics out of a gymnast.

Hockey

- Be Kind to Animals... Hug a Hockey Player
- Chicks with Sticks
- Face Off
- Give Blood... Play Hockey
- Gliding Light
- Hat Trick!
- He/She Shoots—and He/She Scores!
- Here's a Buck, Maybe You Can Buy a Goal!
- Hit Someone... Anyone... Everyone!
- Hitting the Ice
- Hockey Fills My Goal
- Hockey is Life!
- Hockey—Not Just a Game
- Hockeytown!
- Ice Wars
- Icing on the Season
- In the Crease
- Know Hockey, Know Life... No Hockey, No Life...
- My Goal is to Play Hockey
- My Goal is to Deny Yours
- My Other Car is a Zamboni
- On One Blade

SNAPPY SNIPPETS THAT SCORE!

- Penalty Box
- Play for the Glory
- Power Play
- Score!
- Skate Hard... Play Hard... Win Hard!
- Slap Shot
- Slippin' and Slidin'
- Smooth as Glass
- Smooth as Ice
- Sweep the Series
- Clean Sweep
- The Goalie's Best Friend: The Post
- The Hockey Player's Biggest Fan... the Dentist!
- The Puck Stops Here
- Zambonni Man
- A good hockey player plays where the puck is. A great hockey player plays where the puck is going to be. ~ Wayne Gretzky
- Hockey players have fire in their hearts and ice in their veins. ~ Unknown
- Four out of five dentists recommend playing hockey!
- Half the game is mental; the other half is being mental. ~ Jim McKenny

- A puck is a hard rubber disc that hockey players strike when they can't hit one another. ~ Jimmy Cannon
- Hockey is murder on ice. ~ Jim Murray
- Baseball happens to be a game of cumulative tension, but football, basketball and hockey are played with hand grenades and machine guns. ~ John Leonard
- All hockey players are bilingual. They know English and profanity. ~ Gordie Howe
- Hockey players wear numbers because you can't always identify the bodies with dental records.
- By the age of 18, the average American has witnessed 200,000 acts of violence on television, most of them occurring during game 1 of the NHL playoff series. ~ Steve Rushin
- Don't go through life without goals.
- How would you like a job where, every time you make a mistake, a big red light goes on and 18,000 people boo? ~ Jacques Plante
- Hockey is figure skating in a war zone. ~ Unknown

- I skate to where the puck is going to be, not to where it has been. ~ Wayne Gretzky

- Ice hockey is a form of disorderly conduct in which the score is kept. ~ Doug Larson

- High sticking, tripping, slashing, spearing, charging, hooking, fighting, unsportsmanlike conduct, interference, roughing... Everything else is just figure skating. ~ Unknown

- Hockey belongs to the cartoon network, where a person can be pancaked by an Acme anvil, then expanded—accordion style—back to full stature, without any lasting side effect. ~ Steve Rushin

- Hockey captures the essence of Canadian experience in the new world. In a land so inescapably and inhospitably cold, hockey is the chance of life, and an affirmation that despite the deathly chill of winter we are alive. ~ Stephen Leacock

- I went to a fight the other night and a hockey game broke out. ~ Rodney Dangerfield

- When hell freezes over, I'll play hockey there too. ~ Unknown

- Ice hockey players can walk on water. ~ Unknown

- If everyone understood what is really important in life, there would be a shortage of hockey sticks!

- Passing the puck makes bad players good and good players great!

- Street hockey is great for kids. It's energetic, competitive and skilful. And best of all it keeps them off the street. ~ Unknown

- The highest compliment that you can pay me is to say that I work hard every day, that I never dog it. ~ Wayne Gretzky

- There is no one left in Canada who can remember when hockey was a simple game, played for fun. ~ Roy Macgregor

- We get nose jobs all the time in the NHL, and we don't even have to go to the hospital. ~ Brad Park

- You miss 100 percent of the shots you never take. ~ Wayne Gretzky

- I love hockey, and I don't love it for any other reason than when I get out there and play, I enjoy it. ~ Brandon Fehr

Horse Racing

- Another One Bites the Dust
- Around the Turn
- At the Post
- At the Track
- Back in the Saddle Again
- Bailing Out
- Biting the Dust
- Breakneck Speed
- By a Length
- By a Neck
- By a Nose
- By the Rail
- Call to the Post
- Derby Bash
- Derby Day
- Down the Backstretch
- Down to the Wire
- Giddy-Up
- Go, Baby, Go
- Horses Don't Bet on People
- In the Gate
- In the Paddock
- Jockeys on Parade
- Makin' a Move
- On the Turn
- On Track
- Out the Back Door
- Photo Finish
- Placin' a Bet
- Race to the Finish
- Racing Silks
- Ride Like the Wind
- Run for the Roses
- Speak Your Mind, but Ride a Fast Horse
- Splendor in the Bluegrass
- The Starting Gate
- The Winner's Circle
- Triple Crown
- A horse gallops with his lungs, perseveres with his heart, and wins with his character. ~ Tesio
- Anyone who says they made a small fortune in the horse business probably started with a large fortune.
- A horse! A horse! My kingdom for a horse! ~ Shakespeare
- How do you stop this crazy thing?! ~ George Jetson
- The race is not always to the swift, nor the battle to the strong, but that's the way to bet. ~ Damon Runyon

- Money, horse racing and women, three things the boys just can't figure out.
  ~ Will Rogers

- Horse sense is the thing a horse has which keeps it from betting on people.
  ~ W C Fields

- The best horse doesn't always win the race.
  ~ Irish Saying

- I know nothing about racing and any money I put on a horse is a sort of insurance policy to prevent it winning. ~ Frank Richardson

- Any horse can win on any given day. ~ Angel Cordero, Jr.

- The spirited horse, which will try to win the race of its own accord, will run even faster if encouraged.
  ~ Ovid

- Horse racing is animated roulette. ~ Roger Kahn

- Anybody can win unless there happens to be a second entry. ~ George Ade

- Horses and jockeys mature earlier than people—which is why horses are admitted to race tracks at the age of two, and jockeys before they are old enough to shave. ~ Dick Deddoes

- The only sport I'm not interested in is horse racing. That's because I don't know the horses personally. ~ Nat King Cole

- Will is to grace as the horse is to the rider.
  ~ St. Augustine

- They must get to the end and go, "We were just here. What's the point of that?"
  ~ Jerry Seinfeld, on race horses

- The only decent people I ever saw at the racecourse were horses.
  ~ James Joyce

- A horse gallops with his lungs, perseveres with his heart, and wins with his character. ~ Tesio

- A horse is the projection of people's dreams about themselves—strong, powerful, beautiful—and it has the capability of giving us escape from our mundane existence. ~ Pam Brown

- It's a lot like nuts and bolts—if the rider's nuts, the horse bolts!
  ~ The Horse Whisperer

- There are fools, damn fools and those who remount in a steeplechase.
  ~ Bill Whitbread

Horseshoes

- Dead Ringer
- Fever Pitch
- Give Me a Ringer
- Hold Your Horseshoes
- Horsing Around
- Horseshoe Crabs
- Horseshoes: Just Pitch It!
- Horse(shoe) Sense
- A Miss as Good as a Mile
- My Lucky Horseshoe
- Now, That's a Horse(shoe) of a Different Color!
- Pitch In!
- So Close!
- Toss and Turn
- Toss-up
- Happy art thou, as if every day thou hadst picked up a horseshoe. ~ Longfellow
- You can lead a horseshoe to the stake, but you can't make it score.
- Close only counts in horseshoes and grenades. ~ Frank Robinson
- Great American sport. Horseshoes is a very great game. I love it. ~ Dan Quayle

Hot Air Balloon Racing

- Ballooning Hopes
- Full of Hot Air
- Head in the Clouds
- High and Mighty
- High Hopes
- The High Life
- High Spirits
- The Highs and the Lows
- Holding My Head High
- In High Gear
- Into Thin Air
- Into the Wild Blue Yonder
- Magic Carpet Ride
- Natural High
- On the Air
- Out of a Clear Blue Sky
- Sight for "Soar" Eyes
- The Sky's the Limit
- Up-Up and Away
- What Goes up Must Come Down
- The illusion is complete: it seems not to be the balloon that moves, but the earth that sinks down and away... ~ Alberto Santos-Dumont

123

- Flight speaks in different idioms. We can blast rockets to the stars. We can race across the sky on fixed wings. Ballooning appeals because it is more languorous and low-tech; it's adventure in an antique mood. ~ Diane Ackerman

- The balloon seems to stand still in the air while the earth flies past underneath. ~ Alberto Santos Dumont

Hunting

- A-Hunting We Will Go
- Barking Up the Wrong Tree
- The Buck Stops Here
- Cold Turkey
- Future Hunter
- Happy Hunting
- Hunt High and Low
- Hunting is Deer to My Heart
- I'd Rather be Deer Hunting!
- Let's Talk Turkey
- The Old Hunting Ground
- Setting My Sights on Some Good Hunting
- Tag 'Em and Bag 'Em!
- The Thrill of the Hunt
- Wild Goose Chase

- One old hunter and the dear of his life live here.

- Vegetarian is an old Indian word for "bad hunter."

- We interrupt this marriage for hunting season.

- He that hunts two hares will catch neither. ~ Proverb

- Gone huntin'... in pursuit of the elusive white tail!

- The hounds all join in glorious cry, the huntsman winds his horn: and a-hunting we will go. ~ Henry Fielding

- When I die, bury me in the woods... so my husband will hunt for me.

- A hungry dog hunts best. ~ Lee Trevino

- Before beginning a Hunt, it is wise to ask someone what you are looking for before you begin looking for it. ~ Winnie the Pooh

- A hunter will do anything for a buck!

- Gone huntin'... be back at dark thirty!

- Early to bed. Early to rise. Hunt all day. Make up lies.

- Gone huntin'... lookin' for Old Tom!

Ice Dancing

- Anyone Can Dance—It Takes Real Talent to Dance on Ice
- Anyone Can Skate on Ice— It Takes Real Talent to Dance on It
- Crazy Like a Fox(trot)
- Dancing the Blues
- Dancing Up an Ice Storm
- Free Dance: Dance Free
- Ice Age
- Ice Dancing: Cold Ice & Warm Hearts
- Ice Sculptures
- Rhumba: Melting the Ice with Our Passion
- Smooth as Ice
- Takes Two to Tango
- Waltzing onto the Rink
- Smooth ice is paradise for those who dance with expertise. ~ Friedrich Nietzsche
- Ice dance should not be seen as a rigid conformist form of figure skating. There is a great deal of freedom and originality to be had. ~ Robin Cousins
- If you are going to walk on thin ice, you might as well dance.

Lawn Games

- And the Green Grass Grew All Around
- Bag Lady [bean bag toss]
- Bean Bag Toss: It's in the Bag
- Bocce Babe
- Bocce: You Don't Have to be Italian to Love It
- Botched Bocce
- Bowling Inside is for Wimps [lawn bowling]
- Bowling Green [lawn bowling]
- Climbing Jacob's Ladder [ladder ball]
- Dead Ringer [quoits]
- Good Kitty [lawn bowling]
- Great Balls o' Fire
- He/She Don't Know Jack [bocce, lawn bowling]
- Hob Goblin [quoits]
- Hole in One [washers, bean bag toss]
- Just Rolling Along
- Lean on Me [washers]
- Leaner Times [washers]
- Left Holding the Bag [bean bag toss]
- My Sweetie [lawn bowling]

- Roll 'Em
- Queen of Quoits
- Skittles: It Ain't Just a Candy
- Stop, Drop and Egg Roll
- Washed Up Washers
- Washers: Just Pitch It!
- Bean bag... ah, it's very good. Becomes very exciting at times. I saw the championship played in Paris; many people were killed.
  ~ Prescott Chaplin and W.C. Fields
- Old quoits players don't die; they just hole-up.
- Just plain washers. ~ Earle Snell
- The exceptional democratic spirit of the game of Bocce is the basis on which its deeply peaceful character is founded. It is often the beginning of lasting friendships.
  ~ U.S. Bocce Federation
- Old lawn bowlers don't die, they just lose their sweeties.
- It was found that the popularity of the game interfered at times with the security of the state. In other words, the public at large was more interested in playing bocce than in defending their sovereignty!
  ~ Rico Daniele

- Old lawn bowlers don't die, they just get more biased.
- Life isn't all beer and skittles.
  ~ Thomas Hughes
- If you don't play bocce, you don't know jack.
- The only game I've ever played is bean bag.
  ~ Prescott Chaplin and W.C. Fields

Martial Arts

- Above the Belt, Please
- Aikido Aficionado
- Alive and Kicking
- Butterfly Palm
- Eat Your Heart Out, Bruce Lee
- Eight Elbows
- The Family That Kicks Together Sticks Together
- The Gentle Art
- Getting Our Kicks
- I Can Do Tae Kwon Do!
- I Get a Kick from Karate
- I Get a Kick out of You
- It's a Kick
- Jackie Chan's Got Nothing on Me!
- Jitsu Junkie
- Karate Kid

- Kick Back
- Kick It!
- Kick the Habit
- Kung Fu Fighting
- "Ouch!" is Not a Martial Arts Term
- Quest for the Black Belt
- Respect the Rank
- Tae Kwon Do Cutie: I Can Break More Than Hearts
- Talk to the Foot
- Wing Chun: Tan–Bong–Fook
- What a Kick!
- XMA: Extreme Martial Arts
- I come to you with only Karate, Empty Hands. I have no weapons, but should I be forced to defend myself, my principles, or my honor, should it be a matter of life or death, of right or wrong, then here are my weapons, Karate, my Empty Hands. ~ Ed Parker
- It has been said, in regard to a judo expert's level of mental development, that "the arms are an extension of the mind." ~ Watanabe and Avakian
- Audiences always love kung fu. ~ Stephen Chow
- The secret of judo is serenity of mind. ~ Watanabe and Avakian
- Judo rests on flexible action of mind and body. The word flexible, however, never means weakness but something more like adaptability and open-mindedness. Gentleness always overcomes strength. ~ Kyuzo Mifune
- Old martial artists never die; they just lose their kick.
- Tae kwon do: That sharp pain you feel above your head is my foot.
- Follow not in the footsteps of the masters, but rather seek what they sought. ~ Unknown
- People come to practice Tae Kwon Do for different reasons, but my main focus is to keep training to become a top fighter in the nation. ~ Tuong Nguyen
- Thus the principle of Judo, from the very beginning, is not one of aggression, but of flowing with things. ~ Carl B. Becker
- For me, the martial arts is a search for something inside. It's not just a physical discipline. ~ Brandon Lee

- In this way you are able to perfect yourself and contribute something of value to the world. This is the final goal of Judo discipline. ~ Jigoro Kano

- Karate-do is not only the acquisition of certain defensive skills but also the mastering of the arts of being a good and honest member of society. ~ Master Gichin Funakoshi

- My other brother-in-law died. He was a karate expert, then joined the army. The first time he saluted, he killed himself. ~ Henny Youngman

- A black belt is nothing more than a belt that goes around your waist. Being a black belt is a state of mind and attitude. ~ Rick English

- Karate is for life, not points. ~ David Walker

- A punch should stay like a treasure in the sleeve. It should not be used indiscriminately. ~ Master Chotoku Kyan

- Karate is not about winning. It's about not losing. ~ Master Shigetoshi Senaha

- I tried 2x4s, now I pick on things like, Jello. ~ Bill Cosby

- Caution: I know karate... and six other Japanese words!

- Karate is a defensive art from beginning to end. ~ Gichin Funakoshi

- Karate is a form of marital arts in which people who have had years and years of training can, using only their hands and feet, make some of the worst movies in the history of the world. ~ Dave Barry

- No matter how you may excel in the art of karate and in your scholastic endeavors, nothing is more important than your behavior and your humanity as observed in daily life. ~ Master Gichin Funakoshi

- Of those who start tae kwon do training, only about 5% stick with it until they achieve the black belt rank. Then perhaps 80% of those who earn a black stop there. ~ Duk Sung Son

- Karate begins and ends with respect. ~ Master Anko Itosu

- The ultimate aim of karate lies not in victory or defeat but in the perfection of the character of its participants. ~ Gichin Funakoshi

- The teaching of one virtuous person can influence many; that which has been learned well by one generation can be passed on to a hundred.
  ~ Jigoro Kano, founder of Judo

- You may train for a long time, but if you merely move your hands and feet and jump up and down like a puppet, learning karate is not very different from learning a dance. You will never have reached the heart of the matter; you will have failed to grasp the quintessence of karate-do. ~ Gichin Funakoshi

Motorcycle Racing

- And Awaaay She Goes!
- Balancing Act
- Big Wheels Keep on Turnin'
- Biker Babe
- Born to Bike
- Born to Ride My Harley... Forced to Work!
- Breaking Away
- Dirt Roads Teach Patience
- Easy Rider
- First Set of Wheels

- Free Wheelin'
- The Gang's All Here
- Hog Heaven
- It's the Journey
- Keep Those Wheels Rollin'
- Look Mom, No Training Wheels!
- Look Out... Here I Come!
- Makin' Tracks
- Motorcycle Mouth
- Motoring Away
- My Other Car is a Motorcycle
- A Need for Speed
- On a Bike Built for Two
- On Your Mark, Get Set, Go!
- Pedal Practice
- Put the Pedal to the Metal
- Ready, Set, Go!
- Road Hogs
- Round and Around
- Start Your Engines!
- Steady as She Goes
- There's No Looking Back Now!
- Two Wheel Travel
- Un-Easy Rider
- Vroooom!
- Watch Me Go

- Gray-haired riders don't get that way from pure luck.

- Bikes parked out front mean good chicken-fried steak inside.

- Ninety-eight percent of all Harleys ever sold are still on the road. The other two percent made it home.

- A bike on the road is worth two in the shed.

- Born to Ride.
  ~ Harley Davison motto

- Seen on motorcycle rearview mirror—Warning: Objects in mirror are disappearing rapidly.

- A long ride can clear your mind, restore your faith... and use up a lot of fuel.

- Four wheels move the body, two wheels move the soul.

- A motorcycle can't sing on the streets of a city.

- Bikes don't leak oil, they mark their territory.

- If she changes her oil more than she changes her mind—follow her.

- Always replace the cheapest parts first.

- Catching a yellow jacket in your shirt at 70 mph can double your vocabulary.

- A cold hamburger can be reheated quite nicely by strapping it to an exhaust pipe and riding forty miles.

- If you don't ride in the rain—you don't ride.

- There are drunk riders. There are old riders. There are no old, drunk riders.

- When you look down the road, it seems to never end—but you better believe it does.

- But to say that the race is the metaphor for the life is to miss the point. The race is everything. It obliterates whatever isn't racing. Life is the metaphor for the race.
  ~ Donald Antrim

- If you can read this... she fell off! ~ T-Shirt

- Can't wait to get on the road again.

- Saddlebags can never hold everything you want, but they can hold everything you need.

- If you wanna get somewhere before sunset, you can't stop at every tavern.

- Don't lead the pack if you don't know where you're going.

- Don't ride so late into the night that you sleep through the sunrise.

- Where the blacktop ends and the fun begins...

- Home is where your bike sits still long enough to leave a few drops of oil on the ground.

- Never do less than forty miles before breakfast.

- If the person in the next lane at the stoplight rolls up the window and locks the door, support their view of life by snarling at them.

- Most motorcycle problems are caused by the nut that connects the handlebars to the saddle.

- Sometimes the fastest way to get there is to stop for the night.

- What does a Harley and hound dog have in common? They both spend most of their time in the back of a pickup truck. What differentiates the two? The hound dog can get in and out of the pickup under his own power.

- Keep your bike in good repair; motorcycle boots are not comfortable for walking.

- Never argue with a woman holding a torque wrench.

- Never hesitate to ride past the last street light at the edge of town.

- Riding faster than everyone else only guarantees you'll ride alone.

- Never mistake horsepower for staying power.

- Sometimes it takes a whole tankful of fuel before you can think straight.

- The best alarm clock is sunshine on chrome.

- The best modifications cannot be seen from the outside.

- The only good view of a thunderstorm is in your rearview mirror.

- Patience is something you admire in the driver behind you and scorn in the one ahead. ~ Mac McCleary

- Two-lane blacktop isn't a highway—it's an attitude.

- That's all a motorcycle is, a system of concepts worked out in steel. ~ Robert Pirsig

- You can forget what you do for a living when your knees are in the breeze.

- Winter is nature's way of telling you to polish.
- What do you call a cyclist who doesn't wear a helmet? An organ donor. ~ David Perry
- To ride or not to ride... that is a stupid question!
- I believe many Harley guys spend more time revving their engines than actually driving anywhere; I sometimes wonder why they bother to have wheels on their motorcycles. ~ Dave Barry
- Young riders pick a destination and go... old riders pick a direction and go.

Outdoor Water Sports

- All Wet
- Big Skis in a Small Pond
- Blue Water
- Catch a Wave
- Catch the Wind
- Cross Currents
- Down the (Inner) Tube
- Getting His/Her Feet Wet
- Go Jump in a Lake!
- Go with the Flow
- Going Up River
- H$_2$O
- He May Not be a God, but He Walks on Water
- I Do My Own Stunts
- In Deep Water
- Inner (Tube) City
- The Inner (Tube) Circle
- The Inner (Tube) Man/ Woman
- Just Add Water
- Keeping His/Her Head above Water
- Lake District
- Like Water Off a Duck's Back
- Ski Against the Stream
- Ski Me a River
- So Much Water, So Little Time
- Splash!
- Splash Dance
- Still Waters Run Deep
- Testing the Water
- Throw a Tantrum [Wakeboarding]
- Totally Tubular!
- Up a Creek
- Wake Up and Wakeboard!

- Water Party
- Water World
- Wet and Wild
- Wet Behind the Ears (and Everywhere Else!)
- Wet Suit
- If there is magic on this planet, it is contained in water. ~ Loran Eisley
- Our bodies are molded rivers. ~ Novalis
- Water is life's matter and matrix, mother and medium. There is no life without water.
  ~ Albert Szent-Gyorgyi
- Rivers are roads which move, and which carry us whither we desire to go.
  ~ Blaise Pascal
- Old water skiers never die; they just get all washed up.
- The noblest of the elements is water. ~ Pindar
- A lake is the landscape's most beautiful and expressive feature. It is earth's eye; looking into which the beholder measures the depth of his own nature. ~Thoreau
- Water, taken in moderation, cannot hurt anybody. ~ Mark Twain

- It's hard for the modern generation to understand Thoreau, who lived beside a pond but didn't own water skis or a snorkel. ~ Bill Vaughn
- Water, thou hast no taste, no color, no odor; canst not be defined, art relished while ever mysterious. Not necessary to life, but rather life itself, thou fillest us with a gratification that exceeds the delight of the senses.
  ~ Antoine de Saint-Exupery
- You want to be at a pretty good speed, otherwise it's pond swimming rather than skimming. ~ Corie Stone
- A lake carries you into recesses of feeling otherwise impenetrable.
  ~ William Wordsworth
- By the sea—by the sea—by the beautiful sea. ~ Harold Atteridge
- Water is a very good servant, but it is a cruel master. ~ C.G.D. Roberts
- Old ditch-boarders never die, they just get drained.
- You can lead the wakeboarder to water, but you can't get him/her out again.

Parents

- [Sport's name]: As American as Mom and Apple Pie
- [Sport's name] Taxi
- A-Parent Talent
- Can You Say "Sports Scholarship"?
- Daddy's Little (Butt-Kicking) Angel
- Don't You Dare Score Against My Baby!
- Families That Play _____ Together, Stay Together
- He/She Gets It from My Side of the Family
- Hi Mom! Hi Dad!
- I Will Not Embarrass My Child, I Will Not Embarrass My Child...
- Like Father, Like Son
- Like Mother, Like Daughter
- Mama's Boy/Girl
- Minor League Games—Major League Fans
- My Biggest Fans
- My Child Plays _____, Therefore I Have No Life
- My Favorite Player
- My Personal Cheer Team

- No, I am Not Related to the Crazy People in the Stands
- No Kissing. Ma!
- Parents are Chauffeurs, Equipment Managers, Assistant Coaches, and Head Cheerleaders
- Please Ignore Those People in the Stands Shouting My Name
- Soccer Mom/Dad
- Thanks, Mom! Thanks, Dad!
- That's My Baby!
- That's My Boy/Girl!
- Victory Runs in the Family
- We Have No Retirement Fund—Our Child Plays _____
- The only reason we make good role models is because you guys look up to athletes and we can influence you in positive ways. But the real role models should be your parents and teachers!
  ~ Dante Hall
- I mean you got to thank your parents for giving you the right genes.
  ~ Eric Heiden
- We woke up. We played tennis. We brushed our teeth. In that order.
  ~ Andre Agassi

- I went and took golf lessons so Dad would let me play with him. I was just terrible... but I was able to have a wonderful time just walking around with Dad. I can see the real pleasure of that game.
  ~ David Hyde Pierce

- One of the things that my parents have taught me is never listen to other people's expectations.
  ~ Tiger Woods

- Of course I can see better than the referee, I'm a parent!

- When I was 10 or 11, my mom was the one out there catching passes for me. She was my prime receiver. ~ Joe Theismann

- Coaches build teams, parents build players.
  ~ Charles Smyth

- My dad was the force behind me early on. He was just infatuated with baseball. He was the one that basically taught me how to play the game. He gave a lot of his time working out with me, practicing and taking me to a lot of different games. It was hard work between both of us.
  ~ Rafael Palmeiro

- Anyone can be a father, but it takes someone special to be a dad, and that's why I call you dad, because you are so special to me. You taught me the game, and you taught me how to play it right. ~ Wade Boggs

- My mom was at every single game I played as a kid, rain or shine. ~ Ryne Sandberg

- For the parent of a little leaguer, a baseball game is simply a nervous breakdown divided into innings. ~ Earl Wilson

- It's not whether you win or lose—it's how loud your parents cheer.

- My parents influenced me the most. They never played tennis themselves but they were always there and determined, and at times when I wanted to do other stuff they were there to keep me focused and convince me that if I keep on working hard, one day it would pay off and obviously it did. ~ Jana Novotna

- It's the child's desire to play that matters, not the parent's desire to have the child play. Fun. Keep it fun. ~ Tiger Woods

Pool

- Get a Cue!
- Just Lounging Around the Pool (Table)
- Magic Eight Ball
- Odd Balls
- Pool Players Get All the Breaks
- Pool Sharks
- Solids or Striped, I've Got You Wiped
- Stupid Table's Crooked
- Take Your Best Shot!
- That's Your Cue
- I Drool for Pool
- Cue Man
- Think Outside the Pocket
- Break Time
- Rack Runner
- Got Chalk?
- Rack Em' Up!
- Pool Hustler in Training
- Scratch Master
- Straight Shooter
- Every gentleman plays billiards, but someone who plays billiards too well, is no gentleman.
  ~ Thomas Jefferson

- Old pool sharks don't die; they just lose their bite.
- There are six-million shots in the game of pool.
  ~ Albert Einstein
- To play billiards well was a sign of an ill-spent youth.
  ~ Herbert Spencer
- Later on in life it appeared likely that he would have the choice of three professions open to him, namely, professional billiard player, billiard marker, and billiard sharp.
  ~ P.G. Wodehouse
- Old pool players don't die; they just break up.
- The game of billiards has destroyed my naturally sweet disposition.
  ~ Mark Twain
- Anybody who mistreats a pet or breaks a pool cue is docked a month's pay.
  ~ Harpo Marx
- He could play pool for a living and make a living because he's plenty smart.
  ~ Minnesota Fats
- The least thing, such as playing billiards or hitting a ball, is sufficient enough to amuse him. ~ Blaise Pascal
- What happens in the pool hall stays in the pool hall.

136

Referees, Umpires & Game Officials

- Blow the Whistle
- Don't Make Me Blow My Whistle
- Flying the Penalty Flag
- Foul, Really Foul
- I've Earned My Stripes
- Kiss the Ump
- Nobody Loves the Ump
- Red Card
- Refer to the Referee
- Referees Call It Like It is
- Referees Have Seen It All
- Respect the Ref
- Save the Drama for Your Mama
- Thou Shalt Not Take Thy Referee's Name in Vain
- The Umpire Strikes Back
- Whistle-Blower
- World's Best Referee
- Yellow Card
- You Can't Scare Me—I Referee
- Don't park in the spaces marked "Reserved for Umpires." ~ John Mcsherry

- Ideally, the umpire should combine the integrity of a supreme court judge, the physical agility of an acrobat, the endurance of Job and the imperturbability of Buddha. ~ Time Magazine

- It ain't nothin' till I call it. ~ Bill Klem, umpire

- The trouble with referees is that they just don't care which side wins. ~ Tom Canterbury

- Let's face it. Umpiring is not an easy or happy way to make a living. In the abuse they suffer, and the pay they get for it, you see an imbalance that can only be explained by their need to stay close to a game they can't resist. ~ Bob Uecker

- Trying to maintain order during a legalized gang brawl involving 80 toughs with a little whistle, a hanky and a ton of prayer. ~ Anonymous referee, on his job

- I occasionally get birthday cards from fans. But it's often the same message: They hope it's my last. ~ Al Forman, umpire

- Your job is to umpire for the ball and not the player. ~ Bill Klem

- We're supposed to be perfect our first day on the job and show constant improvement.
  ~ Ed Vargo, umpire

- During the opening minutes of a basketball game in which I was involved as a coach, an obvious violation occurred. One of the officials was trying desperately to blow his whistle—but absolutely no sound came out. With a thousand fans howling at him, the hopeless referee inspected his whistle and extracted a small piece of paper from the neck. It was a note, which read: "Good luck tonight. Your loving wife." ~ Unknown

- You can't applaud a referee. ~ Alex Ferguson

Rodeo

- 8 Seconds
- All Tied Up
- Another One Bites the Dust
- At the End of His/Her Rope
- Barrel Racing
- Been There... Rode That...
- Born to Rope... Forced to Work!

- The Buck Stops Here
- Buck Up
- Bucking Bronco
- Bull Riding
- Bull-Headed
- A Bum Steer
- Calf Roping
- Calf Scramble
- CAUTION: Falling Cowboy
- Cow-and-Bull Story
- Cowboy Cadillac
- Cowpokes
- Drugstore Cowboys
- Get Along Lil' Doggies
- Get His/Her Goat
- Gone Ropin'
- Happiness is being a True Cowgirl/boy
- He/She Knows the Ropes
- Hold Your Horses
- Holy Cow!
- King of the Cowboys
- Learning the Ropes
- Making a Quick Buck
- More Bang for Your Buck
- Pass the Buck
- Queen of the Cowgirls

- Ride 'Em Cowboy
- Ride It Out
- Rodeo Champion
- Rodeo Clowns
- Rodeo Girl/Boy in Training
- Rodeo Queen
- Rodeoin' Around
- Rough Ride
- Round 'Em Up
- Seeing Daylight
- Steer Clear
- Steer Wrestling
- Take the Bull by the Horns
- Team Roping
- That's Bull!
- Un-Easy Rider
- Warm-Up Romp
- Wild West
- Wrangler
- There are only three real sports: bull-fighting, car racing and mountain climbing. All the others are mere games. ~ Ernest Hemingway
- Never approach a bull from the front, a horse from the rear, or a fool from any side.
- Courage is being scared to death and saddling up anyway. ~ John Wayne
- Don't squat with your spurs on. ~ Cowboy wisdom
- Because seven is not long enough and nine is too long. ~ Adriano Morales, on why a bull rider must last 8 seconds
- I feel like I've been rode hard and put up wet.
- I'd rather be dumped by a horse than dumped by a man!
- Speak your mind, but ride a fast horse. ~ Cowboy wisdom
- If wishes were horses, beggars would ride.
- I'm so busy... I don't know if I just found a rope or lost my horse.
- It is not enough for a man to know how to ride; he must know how to fall. ~ Mexican Proverb
- A cowboy is a man with guts and a horse. ~ William James
- Riding: The art of keeping a horse between you and the ground.
- When you're young and you fall off a horse, you may break something. When you're my age, you splatter. ~ Roy Rogers

Rugby

- Donate Blood, Play Rugby
- Drop Kick It
- Pile On
- Rough and Ready
- Rugby Hooligans
- Tackle Trouble
- I know that the main scheme is to work the ball down the field somehow and deposit it over the line at the other end and that, in order to squalch this programme, each side is allowed to put in a certain amount of assault and battery and do things to its fellowman which, if done elsewhere, would result in fourteen days without the option, coupled with some strong remarks from the bench. ~ P.G. Wodehouse
- Beer and rugby are more or less synonymous.
  ~ Chris Laidlaw
- The tactical difference between association football and rugby with its varieties seems to be that in the former the ball is the missile, in the latter men are the missiles.
  ~ Alfred E. Crawley

Shooting

- _____, Get Your Gun
- Bite the Bullet
- Bring Out the Big Guns
- I Only Go Shooting on Days Ending with Y
- Jump the Gun
- Just Call Me "Annie Oakley"
- Oh, Shoot!
- Old Eagle-Eye
- Quick-Draw McGraw
- Quick on the Draw
- Setting My Sights on the Prize
- Sharp Shooter
- Shoot 'Em Up
- Shoot from the Hip
- Shooting the Breeze
- A Shot in the Dark
- Silver Bullet
- Smoking Gun
- Son (Daughter) of a Gun!
- Speeding Bullet
- Stick to Your Guns
- Straight from the Shoulder
- Straight Shooter
- Suddenly, a Shot Rang Out!

- Take a Shot
- Trigger Happy
- Trust Me, I'm a Great Shot
- The Whole Shooting Match
- With Guns Blazing
- Aim for the moon. If you miss, you may hit a star. ~ W. Clement Stone
- A good shot lives here with the aim of his life.
- The odds of hitting your target go up dramatically when you aim at it. ~ Mal Pancoast
- Good shots never grow old, they just pick up fewer birds.
- Whatever you are doing, put your whole mind on it. If you are shooting, your mind should be only on the target. Then you will never miss. ~ Swami Vivekananda
- To be sure of hitting the target, shoot first, and call whatever you hit the target. ~ Ashleigh Brilliant
- Skill: What helps you hit the target. Luck: What helps your opponent.
- Thoughts are the gun, words are the bullets, deeds are the target, the bulls-eye is heaven. ~ Doug Horton

- The fascination of shooting as a sport depends almost wholly on whether you are at the right or wrong end of the gun. ~ P. G. Wodehouse
- If I can't go shooting in heaven then I'm not going.
- In the long run, men hit only what they aim at. Therefore, though they should fail immediately, they had better aim at something high. ~ Thoreau

Shuffleboard

- Always Above Board
- It's Time to Go Back the Shuffleboard
- I've Been Framed!
- Just Shuffleboarding Along
- Lost in the Shuffle(board)
- Lucky Puck
- Plucky Pucks
- Shuffleboard Scuffle
- Shuffleboard Superstar
- Sweeping the (Shuffle)Board
- Hockey's for wimps! I play shuffleboard.
- I may be a three on paper, but in my heart I'm a big fat zero.

- I love the idea of a sport you have to be 75 to peak at. ~ Rodney Rothman

- There is more to this sport than just the skill of placing your discs. You have to know how to outwit your opponent. ~ Muriel Rowland

Skating & Skateboarding

- _____ Keeps Getting in My Way!
- Acid Drop
- All Skate
- Alley-Oop
- Backside
- Backwards Only
- Big Spin
- Couples Skate
- Disaster
- Drop In
- Fakie
- Figure Eights
- Flip
- Free Style
- Frontside
- Goofy
- Grand March

- Gravity is a Myth
- Heelflip
- Just a Skater Boy/Girl
- Kickflip
- My Coach Forgot His Whip!
- Nollie
- Ollie
- One-Eighty
- This is How I Roll
- Rink Rat
- Road Rash
- Rock and Roll
- Roll with It
- Rollin'
- Shift Kick
- Skating Through Life
- SK8R
- Three-Sixty
- Trios

- The only way to beat traffic wardens is to take up roller skating. ~ Will Young

- I am not doing spins because with the way they travel I need a passport!

- I have a runny nose. I keep falling over. I have sore feet. My knees are bruised. I am a skater!

- I have recently taken up two new sports: roller skating and ankle spraining, in that order. I am getting quite good at both. ~ Miles Kington

- Old skateboarders never die, they just lose their bearings.

- I put my Olympic gold medal here somewhere and refuse to skate until I find it!

- I consider skateboarding an art form, a lifestyle and a sport. ~ Tony Hawk

- Talent without discipline is like an octopus on roller skates. There's plenty of movement, but you never know if it's going to be forward, backwards, or sideways.
  ~ H. Jackson Brown, Jr.

- I am only doing single jumps because my quad is not working!

- If the good Lord had intended us to walk he wouldn't have invented roller-skates. ~ Willy Wonka

- I keep the tissue industry profitable... I am a skater!

- Want to go traveling? Then why not try one of my spins!

Sky Diving

- Base Jump
- Boogie
- Defying Gravity
- Freestyle
- Free Fallin'
- High Hopes
- Hop-and-Pop
- Into the Wild Blue Yonder
- Jumpmaster
- King/Queen of the Skies
- Natural High
- Skygod
- Swoop
- What Color is Your Parachute?
- What Goes up Must Come Down
- There would be no crowd to watch and applaud my landing. Nor was there any scientific objective to be gained. No, there was deeper reason for wanting to jump, a desire I could not explain.
  ~ Charles Lindbergh

- Plain and simple, skydiving is all about controlled terror, and I love it. ~ Lewis B. Sanborn

- If you go parachuting and your parachute doesn't open and your friends are all watching you fall, I think a funny gag would be to pretend you were swimming.
  ~Jack Handey

- The sky is God's gift to you... what you do with it is your gift to him. ~ Bill Purdin

- Life is either a daring adventure or nothing at all. ~ Helen Keller

- If riding in an airplane is flying, then riding in a boat is swimming. If you want to experience the element, then get out of the vehicle—skydive! ~ Unknown

Sledding

- Across a Winter Wonderland
- All Downhill from Here
- And Awaaay We Go!
- Bob, Bob, Bobsledding Along
- Dashing Through the Snow
- Like Greased Lightning
- A Long Way Down
- Luge Lunge
- Mush! Mush! Good Dog!
- Now Who's Going to Pull Me Back up the Hill?

- Over the Hill
- Over the River and Through the Woods
- Rough Sledding
- Rosebud
- Running Start
- Sled Heads
- Smooth Sledding
- "Snow" Way I'm Stopping!
- Sledding Buddies
- Slippin' and Slidin'
- Basically, I love the sport. It's the combination of physical explosion, running, focusing, hitting a zone... The mental state on a sled feels awesome.
  ~ Katie Uhlaender

- Their tails are high and tongues awag—the twin banners of sled dog contentment. ~ Clara Germani

- When they turn the wind tunnel up to 80 mph, you're not worried about driving the sled, you're not worried about going into or coming out of a curve, you really get a sense of how to have good aerodynamic position. You try picking your head up and you really feel the force. ~ Mark Grimmette

- It's 90 percent mental, and 10 percent physical. It's not hard to lie on the sled.
  ~ Robbie Lyon

- The Happiness of Old Sledders: Once you're over the hill you start to pick up speed.

- Luge strategy? Lie flat and try not to die.
  ~ Carmen Boyle

Snow Skiing & Snowboarding

- All Downhill from Here
- Alpine Angel
- Artic Artist
- Bunny Hill Drop Outs
- Bunny Hill Hang Out
- Catching the Breeze
- Down Hill Racer
- Getting a Lift
- High Hopes
- Hitting the Slopes
- How Do You Walk in These Things?
- How's the Snow?
- I Feel like the Abominable Snowman
- Mogul Mongrel

- Mogul of Moguls
- Powder Puffs
- Ski Bum
- Ski Bunny
- Slippin' and Slidin'
- Smooth as Glass
- The Snow Show
- "Snow" Stopping Now
- Take Me Back to the Lodge—I Need Hot Chocolate
- Warning: Double Black Diamond
- Where are the Brakes?

- Cross country skiing is great if you live in a small country. ~ Steven Wright

- All things are possible—except skiing through a revolving door.

- Heaven seems a little closer when your house is in the mountains.

- I do not participate in any sport with ambulances at the bottom of the hill.
  ~ Erma Bombeck

- It's called "skiing" because "flying" was already taken.

- Powder snow skiing is not fun. It's life, fully lived, life lived in a blaze of reality.
  ~ Dolores Lachapelle

- Skier: One who pays an arm and a leg for the opportunity to break them. ~ Unknown

- Skiing is a dance, and mountain always leads. ~ Unknown

- I think my favorite sport in the Olympics is the one in which you make your way through the snow, you stop, you shoot a gun, and then you continue on. In most of the world, it is known as the biathlon, except in New York City, where it is known as winter. ~ Michael Ventre

- To ski is to travel fast and free—free over untouched snow country... ~ Hans Gmoser

- Skiing: The art of catching cold and going broke while rapidly heading nowhere at great personal risk. ~ Unknown

- Getting an inch of snow is like winning 10 cents in the lottery. ~ Bill Watterson

- The greatest thing that happens to me when I'm skiing is the harmony ... Skiing became the new and healthy way of being present—although I don't know if it's healthy, I could sever my spinal cord. ~ Spalding Gray

- Snowboarding is an activity that is very popular with people who do not feel that regular skiing is lethal enough. ~ Dave Barry

- Mountains have a way of dealing with overconfidence. ~ Hermann Buhl

- Skiing combines outdoor fun with knocking down trees with your face. ~ Dave Barry

- For me, skiing is a physical necessity. I have a need for risk. ~ Jean-Marie Messier

- This is the best place to snowboard, but don't tell anyone. ~ Stacy Kim

- Snowboarding isn't a sport—it's a lifestyle.

- A clever skier will often find an oasis of good snow while the rest of the party ... within a few yards of him ... are struggling with crust. ~ Sir Arnold Lunn

- You're a real skier if your ski gear is worth more than your car.

- The sensual caress of waist deep cold smoke... Glory in skiing virgin snow, in being the first to mark the powder with the signature of their run. ~ Tim Cahill

- There are 206 bones in the human body. No need for dismay, however; the two in the middle ear have never been broken while skiing.

- I now realize that the small hills you see on ski slopes are formed around the bodies of forty-seven-year-olds who tried to learn snowboarding. ~ Dave Barry

- Skiing: When you can't hit the forest for the trees.

- Snow: A form of precipitation that usually occurs three weeks prior to and the morning of your departure from your ski vacation. ~ Unknown

- Stretch pants: The garment that made skiing a spectator sport. ~ Unknown

- The sport of skiing consists of wearing three thousand dollars' worth of clothes and equipment and driving two hundred miles in the snow in order to stand around at a bar and get drunk. ~ P.J. O'rourke

- There are really only three things to learn in skiing: how to put on your skis, how to slide downhill, and how to walk along the hospital corridor. ~ Lord Mancroft

Soccer

- Backyard Soccer
- Black and White and Kicked All Over
- Can I be Goalie?
- Fabulous Forward
- Getting Our Kicks
- Goal!
- Goal, Girl, Goal!
- Great Goal!
- Growling Goalie/Guard
- Hands Off (This is Soccer)
- Happy Feet
- Having a Ball
- He/She Shoots and He/She Scores!
- I Get a Kick out of Soccer
- I Get a Kick out of You
- In a League All Your Own
- Just for Kicks
- Kick Back and Have a Great Time!
- Look, Ma, No Hands!
- Magic Feet
- My Goal is to Play Soccer
- No! Not the Red Card!
- No! The Other Way!

- Penalty Kick
- Play in the Dirt
- Player Down...
- Put Your Head in the Game
- Ready, Set, Goal!
- Run It!
- Score!
- Soccer: A Heady Sensation
- Soccer is a Kick
- Soc(cer) It to Me
- Soccer Kicks
- Soccer Mom/Dad
- Soccer Mom and Proud of It
- Soccer Season
- Soccer—It's Not Just a Game
- Soccer's a Ball!
- Spread Out, Spread Out...
- The True Football!
- Unbelievable End
- Watch Your Offsides!
- What a Kick!
- What Do We Get for Snack?
- Every kid around the world who plays soccer wants to be Pele. I have a great responsibility to show them not just how to be like a soccer player, but how to be like a man. ~ Pele
- Halfback, keeper, forward, defense, offense... I just want to kick the ball!
- The rules of soccer are very simple, basically it is this: If it moves, kick it. If it doesn't move, kick it until it does. ~ Phil Woosnam
- If you're attacking, you don't get as tired as when you're chasing. ~ Kyle Rote Jr.
- In soccer there are no time outs, helmets, shoulder pads, commercial breaks, half time extravaganzas so, if that's what you need... go play football you big wuss! ~ Sara Thomas
- Men play football—intelligent women play soccer!
- Soccer is a game in which everyone does a lot of running around. Twenty-one guys stand around and one guy does a tap dance with the ball. ~ Jim Murray
- Soccer is a sport where the players actually enjoy getting hit in the head by a ball.
- Soccer is simple, but it is difficult to play simple. ~ Johan Cruijff
- My soccer mom can beat up your soccer mom!

- Why is there only one ball for 22 players? If you gave a ball to each of them, they'd stop fighting for it.
- Some say life isn't black and white, mine is.
- When you are out there on the soccer field playing, nothing else matters at the time. It's like the whole world has disappeared, and you and your teammates are all that matters. ~ Amber Massey
- You have got to shoot, otherwise you can't score. ~ Johan Cruijff

Sports (General)

- [School] Scores Big
- [Sport's name] Super Star/Hero
- [Sport's name] is Life, Nothing Else Matters
- [Sport's name] is Life, the Rest is Just Details
- All [area, state, etc.] Team
- All Star
- American Gladiators
- Are You Game?
- Are You Ready for Some [sport's name]?

- Are You Ready to Rumble?
- Armchair Athlete!
- Awards Night
- Beat the Clock
- Big Time Rivalry
- Big Win!
- Catch Some Fun
- Cheer for the Home Team
- Close, but No Prize
- Crashin' the Boards
- Defense! Defense!
- Department of Defense
- Every 1 is a Winner
- Family Game Night
- Faster, Higher, Braver
- Future Olympian
- Game Day
- Game Face
- Game Over
- Games People Play
- Go [school colors]
- Go [team nickname]
- Go for the Gold
- Go Team!
- Go, Team! Fight, Team! Win, Team! Win!
- Good Sports

- Great Game
- Grudge Match
- Have a Field Day
- Havin' a Ball
- Heart of a Champion
- Hero Worship
- Home Team Advantage
- Hooray for Our Team
- I am Woman, See Me Score!
- In a League of Your Own
- Inch by Inch, My Goal's a Cinch
- Instant Replay!
- It's a Real Nail-Bitter!
- It's All in the Game
- It's How You Play the Game
- It's Only a Game till You Lose
- Junior Varsity
- Lions & Tigers & Bears, Oh My!
- My Heroes
- The Sports Page
- Too Close to Call
- Warning: Winning Zone
- We are the Champions
- We Did It!
- If winning isn't everything, why do we keep score? ~ Vince Lombardi

- Is it a life or death game? No, it's far more important than that! ~ Bill Shankly
- We didn't loose the game, we just ran out of time. ~ Vince Lombardi
- A winner is a dreamer who never quits. ~ Unknown
- Winning is a habit, unfortunately so is losing. ~ Vince Lombardi
- The one man team is a complete and total myth. ~ Don Shula
- The more you practice the luckier you get!
- A person really doesn't become whole, until he becomes a part of something that's bigger than himself. ~ Jim Valvano
- The first thing is to love your sport. Never do it to please someone else. It has to be yours. ~ Peggy Fleming
- A winner is someone who recognizes his God-given talents, works his tail off to develop them into skills, and uses these skills to accomplish his goals. ~ Larry Bird
- Always remember, your opponent wants to win as much as you do.

- A winner never quits and a quitter never wins.

- Be more concerned with your character than your reputation. ~ John Wooden

- The main ingredient in stardom is the rest of the team. ~ Unknown

- Champions never complain, they are too busy getting better.

- Drilling, drilling, drilling—we should have hit oil by now!

- Don't tell me how rocky the sea is, just bring in the ship. ~ Vince Lombardi

- Ability will get you to the top, character will keep you there. ~ John Wooden

- Adversity causes some men to break; others to break records. ~ William A. Ward

- Do not let what you cannot do interfere with what you can do. ~ John Wooden

- Every winner has scars and woeful stories of their failures and triumphant stories of their victories. The true winner learns from both. ~ Unknown

- Confidence is contagious. So is the lack of it.
  ~ Vince Lombardi

- The game's isn't over until it's over. ~ Yogi Berra

- It's easy to have faith in yourself and discipline when you're a winner, when you're number 1. What you've got to have is faith and discipline when you are not yet a winner. ~ Vince Lombardi

- An invincible determination can accomplish almost anything, and in this lies the great distinction between great men and little men. ~ Thomas Fuller

- I love to watch the seasons change... football... basketball...hockey...

- Commitment to the team—there is no such thing as in-between, you are either in or out.
  ~ Pat Riley

- Anyone can support a team that is winning—it takes no courage. But to stand behind a team, to defend a team when it is down and really needs you, that takes a lot of courage. ~ Bart Starr

- Everybody on a championship team doesn't get publicity, but everybody can say he's a champion. ~ Magic Johnson

- Discipline is the refining fire which enables talent to become ability.
  ~ John Marcum

- Age is no barrier. It's a limitation you put on your mind. ~ Jakie Joyner-Kersee

- Everyone wants to win, but not everyone is willing to prepare to win. ~ Bobby Knight

- What I spent, I had; what I kept, I lost; what I gave, I have. ~ Henry Ward Beecher

- Fans don't boo nobodies.
  ~ Reggie Jackson

- What to do with a mistake: Recognize it, admit it, learn from it, forget it. ~ Dean Smith

- Extra discipline makes up for a lack of talent and a lack of discipline quickly siphons away extra talent, that's why it's frequently the most disciplined rather than the most gifted rise to the top. ~ Ashur Ashe

- Doubters don't win. Winners don't doubt.

- October is not only a beautiful month but marks the precious yet fleeting overlap of hockey, baseball, basketball, and football. ~ Jason Love

- Win or lose, do it fairly.
  ~ Knute Rockne

- If what you have done yesterday still looks big to you, you haven't done much today. ~ Mike Krzyzewski

- First master the fundamentals. ~ Larry Bird

- I never looked at the consequences of missing a big shot. When you think about the consequences you always think of a negative result. ~ Michael Jordan

- If you practice with emotion and purpose you'll play with passion and confidence.
  ~ Bryan Trottier

- Good is not enough if better is possible.

- I have seen that in any great undertaking, it is not enough for a man to depend simply upon himself. ~ Lone Man

- When you win, nothing hurts. ~ Joe Namath

- The price of success is hard work, dedication to the job at hand, and the determination that whether we win or lose, we have applied the best of ourselves to the task at hand. ~ Vince Lombardi

- In practice, if you don't like to do it, it is probably good for you. ~ D. Cotrell

- The will to win is important, but the will to prepare is vital. ~ Joe Paterno

- There are four seasons: Football season, hockey season, basketball season and baseball season.

- There are two pains in life: The pain of discipline, and the pain of regret. Take your choice.

- Luck is what happens when preparation meets opportunity. ~ Darrel Royal

- I can accept failure, but I can't accept not trying. ~ Michael Jordan

- No one ever says "it's only a game," when their team is winning.

- Individual commitment to a group effort. That's what makes a team work, a company work, a society work, a civilization work. ~ Vince Lombardi

- Lack of confidence is born from a lack of preparation. ~ Shannon Wilburn

- Winning isn't everything, but the will to win is everything. ~ Vince Lombardi

- One player practicing sportsmanship is far better than fifty preaching it. ~ Knute Rockne

- Individually we are special, together we are spectacular.

- Patience and perseverance have a magical effect before which difficulties disappear and obstacles vanish. ~ John Quincy Adams

- Individuals play the game, but teams win championships.

- It ain't over til it's over. ~ Yogi Berra

- Remember this, the choices you make in life, make you. ~ John Wooden

- It takes no talent to hustle. ~ Hans Schmidt

- Keep it simple, when you get too complex you forget the obvious. ~ Al Maguire

- It's not the hours you put in, it's what you put in the hours.

- It's not the push from behind, or the pull from up front, but rather the drive from within. ~ Steve Bankston

- Setting a goal is not the main thing. It is deciding how you will go about achieving it and staying with that plan. ~ Tom Landry

- Winners dwell on their desire, not their limitations. ~ Dr. Dennis Waitley

- It's not bragging if you can do it.

- It's not true that nice guys finish last. Nice guys are winners before the game even starts. ~ Addison Walker

- One finger cannot lift a pebble. ~ Hopi Saying

- Winning is about having the whole team on the same page. ~ Bill Walton

- It's not whether you win or lose, it's all in how you play the game.

- It's rabbit season! No! It's duck season! No! It's [sport's name] season!

- Success is that place in the road where preparation meets opportunity. ~ Branch Rickey

- I've always believed that if you put in the work, the results will come. I don't do things half-heartedly. Because I know if I do, then I can expect half-hearted results. ~ Michael Jordan

- Perfection is not attainable, but if we chase perfection we can catch excellence. ~ Vince Lombardi

- I've missed more than 9000 shots in my career. I've lost almost 300 games. 26 times, I've been trusted to take the game winning shot and missed. I've failed over and over and over again in my life. And that is why I succeed. ~ Michael Jordan

- There may not be an "I" in "team," but there ain't no "we" in it either.

- Teamwork is essential, it gives the enemy someone else to shoot at. ~ Unknown

- Sports do not build character, they reveal it. ~ John Wooden

- If you aren't fired with enthusiasm, then you will be fired with enthusiasm. ~ Vince Lombardi

- Team guts always beat individual greatness. ~ Bob Zuppke

- If you can't win, make the one ahead of you break the record! ~ Jan Mckeithin

- Sports should always be fun. ~ Charles Mann

- Statistically 100% of the shots you don't take don't go in. ~ Wayne Gretsky

- I've/we've got you covered.

- Strive for the excellence it takes to succeed.
- You're never a loser till you quit trying.
- If you can believe it, the mind can achieve it. ~ Ronnie Lott
- Sweet smell of victory— and stinky socks!
- If you don't practice, you don't deserve to dream.
- The difference between an extraordinary player and an ordinary player is that little extra. ~ Michael Burks
- Be humble in victory and gracious in defeat.
- If you think small things don't matter, think of the last game you lost by one point.
- I've/we've got your back.
- Teamwork means never having to take all the blame yourself.
- Work hard to make things easier. ~ Pete Carill
- There are two things in life: [sport's name] and more [sport's name].
- You can only win if you aren't afraid to lose.
- Winning isn't everything, it's the only thing. ~ Vince Lombardi

- The difference between a successful person and others is not a lack of strength, not lack of knowledge, but rather a lack of will. ~ Vince Lombardi
- Victory goes to the player who makes the next-to-the-last mistake. ~ Unknown
- The essence of sports is that while you're doing it, nothing else matters. But after you stop, there is a place, generally not very important, where you put it. ~ Roger Bannister
- There is only one way to succeed in anything, and that is to give it everything. ~ Vince Lombardi
- Ask any athlete: We all hurt at times. I'm asking my body to go through seven different tasks. To ask it not to ache would be too much. ~ Jakie Joyner-Kersee
- You have to expect things of yourself before you can do them. ~ Michael Jordan
- We are not going to play them; they are going to play us. ~ Hank Iba
- You are only defeated if you give up one more time than you get up. ~ Unknown

- Think and then act. Never act and then alibi. ~ Hank Iba

- Your toughest competition in life is anyone who is willing to work harder than you. ~ Casey Coleman

- Ask not what your teammates can do for you. Ask what you can do for your teammates. ~ Magic Johnson

- To be successful, you don't have to do extraordinary things. Just do ordinary things extraordinarily well. ~ John Rohn

- You don't demand respect, you earn it. ~ Steve Seidler

- Victory or defeat is not determined at the moment of crisis, but rather in the long and unspectacular period of preparation. ~ Unknown

- Champions aren't made in the gyms. Champions are made from something they have deep inside them—a desire, a dream, a vision. ~ Muhammad Ali

- Hate to boast, but I caught the most.

- Losers live in the past. Winners learn from the past. ~ Denis Waitley

- You can accomplish anything you want as long as you don't care who gets the credit for it. ~ Blanton Collier

- To win, all you have to do is get up one more time than you fall. ~ Unknown

- You can't hit a home run unless you step up to the plate. ~ Kathy Seligman

- Victory is sweetest when you've known defeat.

- You're never as good as everyone tells you when you win and you're never as bad as they say when you lose. ~ Lou Holtz

Surfing

- All Wet
- Baggies [surf shorts]
- Barrel
- Beach Break
- Beach Bums
- The Big Wave
- Blown Out
- Blue Water
- Catch a Wave
- Catch the Wind
- Closed Out
- Cowabunga!

- Getting Their Feet Wet
- Getting Some Air
- Gnarly, Bro'
- Go with the Flow
- H_2O
- Hang Ten
- He May Not be a God, but He Walks on Water
- Highwave Patrol
- Making a Splash
- Making Waves
- Pearl
- Reef Break
- Soul Surfer
- Surf Music
- Surf's Up
- Surfer Dude
- Short Board
- Shred It!
- Time & Tide Wait for No Man/Woman
- Water World
- Wave Reviews
- Wet and Wild
- Wipeout!
- You can't stop the waves, but you can learn to surf. ~ Jon Kabat-Zinn

- Surfing is such an amazing concept. You're taking on Nature with a little stick and saying, "I'm gonna ride you!" And a lot of times Nature says, "No you're not!" and crashes you to the bottom. ~ Jolene Blalock

- The rest of the world disappears for me when I'm on a wave. ~ Paul Walker

- As for my own surfing, let's just say that when the waves start pushing 10 feet, I get this tremendous urge to make a sandwich. ~ Bruce Jenkins

- There's no sport, that I know of, that has all the ingredients of pure enjoyment that surfing does. Don't ever take yourself too seriously out there, just have fun. ~ Peter Cole

- How would you like to stand like a god before the crest of a monster billow, always rushing to the bottom of a hill and never reaching its base, and to come rushing in for a half mile at express speed, in graceful attitude, until you reach the beach and step easily from the wave? ~ Duke Kahanamoku

- Sometimes in the morning, when it's a good surf, I go out there, and I don't feel like it's a bad world. ~ Kary Mullis

- I could not help concluding this man had the most supreme pleasure while he was driven so fast and so smoothly by the sea.
  ~ James Cook

- One of the greatest things about the sport of surfing is that you need only three things: your body, a surf-board, and a wave. ~ Naima Green

Swimming

- Ahoy, Mateys!
- All is Calm, All is Bright
- All Wet
- As Still as Glass
- Belly Flop!
- Beneath the Surface
- Blue Water
- Butterflies
  [butterfly embellishments]
- Chlorine is My Perfume
- Coolin' Off in the Pool
- Cross Currents
- A Day at the Races

- Dive Right In
- Drenched
- Eat My Bubbles
- Everything's Going Swimmingly
- A Floatin' Party
- Full Steam Ahead
- Getting Their Feet Wet
- Go with the Flow
- H_2O
- Hair-larious [wet hair]
- High Divin' Daredevil
- A Human Cannonball
- In the Swim of Things
- Junior Lifeguard
- Just Add Water
- Just Floatin' Along
- Just Keepin' My Head above Water
- Kerplunk! Kersplash!
- Lifeguard in Training!
- Making a Splash in the World
- Making Fishy Faces
- Making Waves
- Marco Polo
- A Need for Speed
- On the Ropes

- On Your Mark, Get Set, Go!
- Our Little Fish
- Oxygen is Overrated
- Pool School
- Pool-ish Pleasures
- Poolside Pals
- Sink or Swim
- Skinny Dipper
- Sliding into Fun
- Soaking Wet
- Splash!
- Splash Dance
- Splash Down
- Splashing the Day Away
- Splish! Splash!
- Stayin' Afloat
- Sun-Bathing Beauty
- Swimming in the Fast Lane
- Swimming Lessons
- Takin' a Dip
- Taking the Plunge
- Testing the Waters
- The Jewel of the Pool
- The Little Mermaid
- The Swimsuit Edition
- The Unsinkable [Molly Brown]
- Three Little Fishes

- Treading Water
- Underwater Fun
- Water Party
- Water Wars
- Water World
- Wave Reviews
- Wet 'n' Wild
- You Rule the Pool
- If one synchronized swimmer drowns, do all the rest have to drown too?
  ~ Steven Wright
- Chlorine: the breakfast of champions! ~ Unknown
- If I were dropped out of a plane into the ocean and told the nearest land was a thousand miles away, I'd still swim. And I'd despise the one who gave up.
  ~ Abraham Maslow
- H_2O: Two parts heart and one part obsession.
- If you should rear a duck in the heart of the Sahara, no doubt it would swim if you brought it to the Nile.
  ~ Mark Twain
- If the world was flat I'd probably swim off it.
- Live in the sunshine, swim the sea, drink the wild air.
  ~ Ralph Waldo Emerson

- If you have a lane, you have a chance. ~ Unknown

- Don't wait for your ship to come in—swim out to it.

- It's a good idea to begin at the bottom in everything except in learning to swim. ~ Unknown

- Seventy-five percent of our planet is water—can you swim?

- I can't fly, but swimming is the next best thing... the water is my sky. ~ Unknown

- It's been told that swimming is a wimp sport, but I don't see it. We don't get timeouts, in the middle of a race we can't stop and catch our breath, we can't roll on our stomachs and lie there, and we can't ask for a substitution. ~ Unknown

- Remember, a dead fish can float downstream, but it takes a live one to swim upstream. ~ Unknown

- I simply can't understand why swimsuits are in such demand they're soggy and damp, bind like a clamp and hold about three pounds of sand! ~ D.R. Benson

- Seven days of no swimming makes one weak. ~ Unknown

- If you want to learn to swim, jump into the water. On dry land no frame of mind is ever going to help you. ~ Bruce Lee

- Sometimes God calms the storm. At other times, He calms the sailor. And sometimes He makes us swim. ~ Unknown

- Most of us, swimming against the tides of trouble the world knows nothing about, need only a bit of praise or encouragement—and we will make the goal. ~attrib. to Jerome Fleishman & Robert Collier

- No man drowns if he perseveres in praying to God and can swim. ~ Russian Proverb

- By the sea—by the sea—by the beautiful sea. ~ Harold Atteridge

- Well, me don't swim too tough, so me don't go in the water too deep. ~ Bob Marley

- Swimming: From the outside looking in, you can't understand it. From the inside looking out, you can't explain it. ~ Unknown

- What goes around comes around, just like a flip turn.

- When the earth floods from global warming, swimmers will rule the world.

- Doing is a quantum leap from imagining. Thinking about swimming isn't much like actually getting in the water. Actually getting in the water can take your breath away. The defense force inside of us wants us to be cautious, to stay away from anything as intense as a new kind of action... But it's often wrong. ~ Barbara Sher

- The water is your friend. You don't have to fight with water, just share the same spirit as the water, and it will help you move. ~ Aleksandr Popov

- My mom said she learned how to school when someone took her out in the lake and threw her off the boat. I said, "Mom, they weren't trying to teach you how to swim." ~ Paula Poundstone

- The man who is swimming against the stream knows the strength of it. ~ Woodrow T. Wilson

- Swimming—what real men do while boys play football.

Table Tennis & Ping Pong

- Are You Being Served?
- Eat. Sleep. Play Table Tennis.
- Happy to Serve
- King/Queen Pong
- My Game, My Table, Your Loss
- My Sweet Spot
- Ping Pong Diplomacy
- Ping Pong: Not for the Timid!
- No Paddle, No Battle
- Table Tennis Rocks!
- Table Tennis is My World!
- Warning: Table Tennis Zone

- The extreme sport I play is ping pong. And we play it hard. If any of you suckers want to step up to the table, be ready. ~ Seth Green

- In other parts of the world, table tennis is taken very seriously. In North America ... it's referred to as "ping pong." ~ Sean Hilliker

- If there's no table tennis in heaven, I'm not going.

- Playing table tennis is not a matter of life or death—its much more important than that.

Tennis

- 40–Love
- Clear the Net!
- Don't Argue with the Line Judge!
- Game after Game, I'm Having Fun
- Going to Court
- It's Over!
- It's Out!
- King/Queen of the Court
- Love Hurts
- Love Tennis!
- My Purpose is in Life to Serve Others
- Over the Net!
- Point-Set-Match
- Smash It!
- Tenacious Tennis Player
- Tennis Anyone?
- Tennis Bum
- Tennis: Gotta Love It!
- Tennis—It's Not Just a Game
- Tennis Menace
- Tennis is My Racquet
- What a Racquet!
- Wimbledon, Here I Come

- If you can react the same way to winning and losing, that's a big accomplishment. Quality is important because it stays with you the rest of your life, and there's going to be a life after tennis that's a lot longer than your tennis life.
  ~ Chris Evert Lloyd

- Tennis belongs to the individualistic past—a hero, or at most a pair of friends or lovers, against the world. ~ Jacques Barzun

- Champions keep playing until they get it right.
  ~ Billie Jean King

- What a polite game tennis is. The chief word in it seems to be "sorry" and admiration of each other's play crosses the net as frequently as the ball.
  ~ J.M. Barrie

- An otherwise happily married couple may turn a mixed doubles game into a scene from Who's Afraid of Virginia Woolf.
  ~ Rod Laver

- When I was 40, my doctor advised me that a man in his 40s shouldn't play tennis. I heeded his advice carefully and could hardly wait until I reached 50 to start again. ~ Hugo L. Black

- Tennis is an addiction that once it has truly hooked a man will not let him go.
  ~ Russell Lynes

- But that won't give me a free hand to hold the beer.
  ~ Billy Carter, on a two-handed backhand shot

- A perfect combination of violent action taking place in an atmosphere of total tranquility. ~ Billie Jean King

- It's one-on-one out there, man. There ain't no hiding. I can't pass the ball.
  ~ Pete Sampras

- Love is nothing in tennis, but in life it's everything.

- In tennis the addict moves about a hard rectangle and seeks to ambush a fuzzy ball with a modified snow-shoe. ~ Elliot Chaze

- "Good shot," "bad luck" and "hell" are the five basic words to be used in a game of tennis, though these, of course, can be slightly amplified. ~ Virginia Graham

- I have always considered tennis as a combat in an arena between two gladiators who have their racquets and their courage as their weapons.
  ~ Yannick Noah

- It's difficult for most people to imagine the creative process in tennis. Seemingly it's just an athletic matter of hitting the ball consistently well within the boundaries of the court. That analysis is just as specious as thinking that the difficulty in portraying King Lear on stage is learning all the lines. ~ Virginia Wade

- I'll let the racket do the talking. ~ John Mcenroe

- Speed in tennis is a strange mixture of intuition, guesswork, footwork and hair-trigger reflexes.
  ~ Eugene Scott

- The serve was invented so that the net could play.
  ~ Bill Cosby

- Tennis is more than just a sport. It's an art, like the ballet. Or like a performance in the theater. When I step on the court I feel like Anna Pavlov, or like Adeline Patti, or even like Sarah Bernhard. I see the footlights in front of me. I hear the whisperings of the audience. I feel an icy shudder. Win or die! Now or never! It's the crisis of my life. ~ Bill Tilden

- Tennis matches always begin with love.

- Tennis: A racquet sport in which two players compete to see who has the shortest temper, the worst memory, the poorest eyesight, and the slowest watch. ~ Unknown

- Tennis players love getting into the swing of things!

- The cunning competitor plays on the other party's guilt. Continuously praise your opponent's shots, and you'll notice how he begins to press. Self-beratement also serves to balance a guilty conscience for being successful and makes your opponent disturbed for upsetting you so. ~ Theodor Saretsky

- The primary conception of tennis is to get the ball over the net and at the same time to keep it within bounds of the court; failing this, within the borders of the neighborhood.
  ~ Elliot Chaze

- The depressing thing about tennis is that no matter how good I get, I'll never be as good as a wall.
  ~ Mitch Hedberg

- When you lose a couple of times, it makes you realize how difficult it is to win.
  ~ Steffi Graf

- I can't really play—I just love the outfits.

- Why has slamming a ball with a racquet become so obsessive a pleasure for so many of us? It seems clear to me that a primary attraction of the sport is the opportunity it gives to release aggression physically without being arrested for felonious assault. ~ Nat Hentoff

- Tennis is not a gentle game.
  ~ Richard Evans

- Though your game is hardly the best, you can fray your opponent's nerves by methodically bouncing the ball at least ten times before your serves. ~ Arnold J. Zarett

- If on occasion you call one of your opponent's "out" shots "in," then later on you can innocently call an "in" shot "out" on a crucial play. Practice saying "good try," sincerely; then you can call a lot of close shots "out" and get away with it. ~ Theodor Saretsky

Track & Field

- [10]K Marathon
- 1, 2, 3 Jump!
- A Day at the Races
- And They're Off!
- Back on Track
- Big Shot (Put)
- Born to Run
- Camptown Races
- Chariots of Fire
- Darth Vaulter [pole vault]
- Dash of Excitement
- Discus Dizzies
- Eat My Dust!
- Finishers are Winners
- Get Ready, Get Set, Go!
- Giant Leap
- Give It a Shot (Put)
- Going the Distance
- Hammer It Home
- Hammer the Competition [hammer throw]
- Have a Field Day
- High Hopes [pole vault, high jump]
- High Hurdles
- I Can Go the Distance
- I'm Running for My Life
- In the Running
- Jaunty Javelins
- Jump for Joy [high jump]
- Jumpin' Jehoshaphat [high jump]
- Just (Shot) Puttering Around
- Leapin' Lizards [high jump]
- Life in the Fast Lane
- Life in the Slow Lane
- Long, Long, Long Distance
- The Long Run
- Makin' Tracks
- My Sport is Your Sport's Punishment
- A Need for Speed
- Off and Running
- On the Fast Track
- On Track
- On Your Mark, Get Set, Go!
- One Giant Leap for a Man
- One Track Mind
- Outpaced
- Overcoming Hurdles
- Photo Finish
- Poles Apart [pole vault]
- Putting a Positive Spin on Things [discus, shot put]

- The Race is On
- Race to the Finish
- Ready, Set, Go!
- Riches in the (Pole) Vault
- Round & Round & Round He/She Goes [discus, shot put]
- Run, _____, Run
- Run for Your Life
- Running Like the Wind
- Slow & Steady Wins the Race
- Sprint to the Finish
- Thor's Hammer [hammer throw]
- Throw It Down [hammer throw, discus, etc.]
- Too Far to Find
- Under the Hammer [hammer throw]
- Where Did It Go? [javelin]
- Who Will You Run to?
- Everyone in life is looking for a certain rush. Racing is where I get mine.
  ~ John Trautmann
- Blink and you miss a sprint. The 10,000 meters is lap after lap of waiting. Theatrically, the mile is just the right length—beginning, middle, end: a story unfolding.
  ~ Sebastian Coe
- Chase after the truth like all hell and you'll free yourself, even though you never touch its coat-tails.
  ~ Clarence S. Darrow
- Doctors and scientists said that breaking the four-minute mile was impossible, that one would die in the attempt. Thus, when I got up from the track after collapsing at the finish line, I figured I was dead.
  ~ Roger Bannister, 1st person to break the 4-minute mile
- An athlete cannot run with money in his pockets. He must run with hope in his heart and dreams in his head. ~ Emil Zatopek
- I love the feeling of freedom in running, the fresh air, the feeling that the only person I'm competing with is me.
  ~ Wilma Rudolph
- Everyone who has run knows that its most important value is in removing tension and allowing a release from whatever other cares the day may bring. ~ Jimmy Carter
- I'd never be able to run that far. ~ Scott Adams
- First is first, and second is nowhere. ~ Ian Stewart

- Even if you fall flat on your face, at least you are moving forward. ~ Sue Luke

- Begin at the beginning and go on till you come to the end; then stop. ~ Lewis Carroll

- If the hill has its own name, then it's probably a pretty tough hill. ~ Marty Stern

- For most of us, a marathon is less a race than a survival test. The big question before a shorter race is, "how fast will I finish?" the big one before a marathon is, "will I finish at all?"
  ~ Joe Henderson

- If you can't win, make the fellow ahead of you break the record. ~ Unknown

- No one can say, "You must not run faster than this, or jump higher than that." The human spirit is indomitable.
  ~ Sir Roger Bannister

- I always loved running... it was something you could do by yourself, and under your own power. You could go in any direction, fast or slow as you wanted, fighting the wind if you felt like it, seeking out new sights just on the strength of your feet and the courage of your lungs. ~ Jesse Owens

- I ran and ran every day, and I acquired a sense of determination, this sense of spirit that I would never, never, give up, no matter what else happened. ~ Wilma Rudolph

- Most mistakes in a race are made in the first two minutes, perhaps in the very first minute.
  ~ Coach Jack Daniels

- If God invented marathons to keep people from doing anything more stupid, the triathlon must have taken him completely by surprise.
  ~ P.Z. Pearce

- No doubt a brain and some shoes are essential for marathon success, although if it comes down to a choice, pick the shoes. More people finish marathons with no brains than with no shoes. ~ Don Kardong

- There is an itch in runners.
  ~ Arnold Hano

- Why couldn't Pheidippides have died here?
  ~ Frank Shorter, at the 16 mile mark of a marathon

- There will come a point in the race, when you alone will need to decide. You will need to make a choice. Do you really want it? ~ Rolf Arands

- It's better to burn out than to fade away. ~ Tom Petty

- Most people never run far enough on their first wind to find out they've got a second. ~ William James

- Only think of two things: The gun and the tape. When you hear the one, just run like hell until you break the other.
  ~ Sam Mussabini

- Thank God, it's over.
  ~ Neil Cusack

- Most people run a race to see who is fastest. I run a race to see who has the most guts. ~Steve Prefontaine

- Runners just do it—they run for the finish line even if someone else has reached it first. ~ Unknown

- My thoughts before a big race are usually pretty simple. I tell myself: "Get out of the blocks, run your race, stay relaxed. If you run your race, you'll win... channel your energy. Focus." ~ Carl Lewis

- Nothing splendid has ever been achieved except by those who dared believe that something inside them was superior to circumstance. ~ Bruce Barton

- Pain is weakness leaving the body. ~ Tom Sobal

- Running is a road to self-awareness and self-reliance... you can push yourself to extremes and learn the harsh reality of your physical and mental limitations or coast quietly down a solitary path watching the earth spin beneath your feet. But when you are through, exhilarated and exhausted, at least for a moment everything seems right with the world. ~ Unknown

- The difference between the mile and the marathon is the difference between burning your fingers with a match and being slowly roasted over hot coals.
  ~ Hal Higdon

- I don't think the discus will ever attract any interest until they let us start throwing them at each other. ~ Al Oerter

- The man who can drive himself further once the effort gets painful is the man who will win.
  ~ Sir Roger Bannister

- Run like hell and get the agony over with.
  ~ Clarence Demar

- To a runner, a side stitch is like a car alarm. It signifies something is wrong, but you ignore it until it goes away.
  ~ Unknown

- I competed in the high jump in high school, but I wasn't very good. My technique was to stand around looking intimidating because I was so tall.
  ~ Geena Davis

- The start of a world cross country event is like riding a horse in the middle of a buffalo stampede. It's a thrill if you keep up, but one slip and you're nothing but hoof prints. ~ Ed Eyestone

- I don't compete with other discus throwers. I compete with my own history.
  ~ Al Oerter

- The gun goes off and everything changes... the world changes... and nothing else really matters.
  ~ Patti Sue Plummer

- The hardest part of the marathon is the training. Race day is graduation day, when you celebrate with fellow graduates and supporters who've helped you come this far.
  ~ Joe Henderson

- It's unnatural for people to run around the city streets unless they are thieves or victims. It makes people nervous to see someone running. I know that when I see someone running on my street, my instincts tell me to let the dog go after him. ~ Mike Royko

- There's no such thing as bad weather, just soft people. ~ Bill Bowerman

- We are different, in essence, from other men. If you want to win something, run 100 meters. If you want to experience something, run a marathon. ~ Emil Zapotek

- To describe the agony of a marathon to someone who's never run it is like trying to explain color to someone who was born blind. ~ Jerome Drayton

- You don't run against a bloody stop watch, do you hear? A runner runs against himself, against the best that's in him. Not against a dead thing of wheels and pulleys. That's the way to be great, running against yourself. Against all the rotten mess in the world.
  ~ Bill Persons

• The strategy of my coach and me was that we looked at pictures of all the best pole vaulters from around the world, and we took the best parts from them, and we created a person that had never existed. We then started to work toward being such a person.
~ Sergei Bubka

• There are as many reasons for running as there are days in the year, years in my life. But mostly I run because I am an animal and a child, an artist and a saint. So, too, are you. Find your own play, your own self-renewing compulsion, and you will become the person you are meant to be.
~ George Sheehan

• There is no time to think about how much I hurt; there is only time to run.
~ Ben Logsdon

• Don't count all the runners ahead of you and feel intimidated. Instead look back proudly at all those you're leading, especially those you can't see because they never reached the starting line.
~ Joe Henderson

Trampoline

• The Boiiiing Brothers

• Bouncing Back

• Break the Egg

• Butt Wars

• Fun You Can Flip Over

• High Hopes

• Jump for Joy

• Jump'n Jehoshaphat

• Jump'n Jacks

• Jump-o-line

• Leapin' Lizards

• One Giant Leap for Mankind

• Life is a cement trampoline.
~ Howard Nordberg

• If you could build a house on a trampoline, that would suit me fine. ~ Alan Rickman

• Success is how high you bounce when you hit the bottom. ~ General Patton

• If they ever come up with a Swashbuckling School, I think one of the courses should be Laughing, Then Jumping Off Something.
~ Jack Handey

• Jump, and you will find how to unfold your wings as you fall. ~ Ray Bradbury

Unicycle

- Big Wheel Keeps on Rolling
- Look, Ma, No Hands!
- Just Rollin' Along
- MUni Madness
- MUni: Rockin' & Rollin'
- One with the Wheel
- Ride a Bicycle? I Don't Need a Training Wheel!
- This is How I Roll
- Unicycle: A Bike Without All the Useless Stuff
- Unicyclists are Wheel-y Wonderful
- Unicyclists, Unite!
- Unique Cyclists
- What's the 2nd Wheel for?
- Where There's a Wheel, There's a Way
- No gears, no brakes, no handlebars... no problem!
  ~ T-shirt
- I took lessons in bicycle riding. But I could only afford half of them. Now I can ride a unicycle.
  ~ Steven Wright
- I was kind of bored with mountain biking, so I took my old unicycle out.
  ~ David Orchard
- A lot of people will try and never stick with it long enough. Most people could ride a unicycle if they stuck with it for a week or two. It's amazing how people will go by and honk and wave and stop a lot. If you were on a skateboard, even if you were really good, you wouldn't get that kind of attention.
  ~ Barry Hotrum
- It takes twice the man/woman to ride half the bike.
- Any place a mountain bike can go, a mountain unicycle can go. ~ John Drummond

Volleyball

- All Set
- Are You Being Served?
- Block This!
- Bump! Set! Spike!
- Clear the Net!
- Eager to Serve
- Free Ball!
- Free Facials
- Havin' a Ball
- Love at First Spike
- Over the Net!
- Dig It Up, Slam It Down!

- Diggin' & Divin'
- Get Your Ace in Gear
- It's Over!
- It's Out!
- I've Got an Ace Up My Sleeve
- Jump Serve
- King/Queen of the Court
- Kiss My Ace
- Mine!
- Mr. Sandman
- Net Attack
- Net Force
- See You in Court
- Set Up!
- Slam!
- Spike!
- That One's Yours!
- An Underhanded Deed
- Up and Over
- Volley Girls
- Volleyball—Not Just a Game
- What a Dig!
- What a Volley!
- What Goes up Must Come Down
- Volleyball is my passion. It's what makes me go.
  ~ Gabrielle Reese

- If volleyball was easy, they would have called it "football."
- My "weak side" is still stronger than your "strong side."
- The only reason I go to school is to play volleyball.
- Excuse me, you don't dig the ball with your face!
- You touch every other ball and, if you screw up, you only have one more person to back you up. You can't go hide in the corner.
  ~ Kerri Walsh, on indoor vs. beach volleyball
- There is pressure on every play. You can't make a mistake, but that also means your opponent can't make a mistake. It makes the matches more exciting to watch. ~ Holly Mcpeak
- I hope your game is as tight as your spandex.
- Beach volleyball, n.: An activity which takes place in a calm, peaceful beach setting, and which resembles a full-scale war.
- The setter: A hard working talented volleyball player who receives no glory!
  ~ T-Shirt

- Eat, sleep volleyball... is there anything else?

- Hot hands, great legs, killer attitude! (Don't mess with the best.) ~ T-Shirt

- It takes a lot of hard work and dedication just like any pro sport. Especially for beach volleyball you don't have to be tall or as fast as other sports. You just have to have the skills. ~ Misty May

- To some it's a hobby; to others it's a sport—to me it's an obsession.

Walking, Jogging, & Running

- Born to Run
- Don't Run Out on Me
- Feel the Burn
- Give You the Run-Around
- Gonna Walk All Over You
- I Can Run Circles Around You
- I Often Go Walking
- I Ran Before I Could Walk
- I'm Running for My Life
- Jog My Memory—Why Do I Do This Again?
- Just Jogging Along

- Live to Run, Run to Live
- The Long Run
- Makin' Tracks
- My Walk of Life
- Off and Running
- One Track Mind
- The Race is On
- Roadwork
- Run Away with Me
- Run Down
- Run a Fever
- Run Out of Patience
- Run Ragged
- Run Rampant
- Run the Gauntlet
- Run the Good Race
- Run Wild
- Running Like the Wind
- Running Sets Me Free
- Running with the Big Dogs
- Shut Up and Run
- Slow and Steady Wins the Race
- Take a Hike
- Track Runs in the Family
- Walk Forever by My Side
- Walk Tall
- Walk the Plank

- Walk the Walk
- Walking a Thin Line
- Walking on Air
- Walking on Eggshells
- We'll Have the Competition Running Scared
- Who Will You Run To?
- Why are You All Chasing Me?
- Your Mark, Get Set, Go
- We live with our heels as well as head and most of our pleasure comes in that way. ~ John Muir
- Don't let people drive you crazy when you know it's in walking distance. ~ Unknown
- A dog is one of the remaining reasons why some people can be persuaded to go for a walk. ~ O.A. Battista
- Hiking is the best workout! You can hike for three hours and not even realize you're working out. And, hiking alone lets me have some time to myself.
  ~ Jamie Luner
- As a nation we are dedicated to keeping physically fit—and parking as close to the stadium as possible. ~ Bill Vaughan
- A pedestrian is someone who thought there were a couple of gallons left in the tank. ~ Unknown
- A vigorous five-mile walk will do more good for an unhappy but otherwise healthy adult than all the medicine and psychology in the world. ~ Paul Dudley White
- At mile 20, I thought I was dead; at mile 22, I wished I was dead; at mile 24, I knew I was dead; at mile 26.2 I knew I had become too tough to kill. ~ Unknown
- Above all, do not lose your desire to walk. Every day I walk myself into a state of well-being and walk away from every illness. I have walked myself into my best thoughts, and I know of no thought so burdensome that one cannot walk away from it.
  ~ Søren Kierkegaard
- Climb the mountains and get their good tidings. Nature's peace will flow into you as sunshine flows into trees. The winds will blow their own freshness into you, and the storms their energy, while cares will drop off like autumn leaves. ~ John Muir

- In every walk with nature one receives far more than he seeks. ~ John Muir

- I have two doctors, my left leg and my right.
  ~ G.M. Trevelyan

- After a day's walk everything has twice its usual value.
  ~ George Macauley Trevelyan

- Everywhere is walking distance if you have the time. ~ Steven Wright

- After dinner sit awhile, after supper walk a mile.
  ~ English Proverb

- An early-morning walk is a blessing for the whole day.
  ~ Thoreau

- If I could not walk far and fast, I think I should just explode and perish.
  ~ Charles Dickens

- How can you explain that you need to know that the trees are still there, and the hills and the sky? Anyone knows they are. How can you say it is time your pulse responded to another rhythm, the rhythm of the day and the season instead of the hour and the minute? No, you cannot explain. So you walk. ~ New York Times

- I still find each day too short for all the thoughts I want to think, all the walks I want to take, all the books I want to read and all the friends I want to see. ~ John Burroughs

- He who limps is still walking.
  ~Stanislaw J. Lec

- I don't think jogging is healthy, especially morning jogging. If morning joggers knew how tempting they looked to morning motorists, they would stay home and do sit-ups. ~ Rita Rudner

- I dream of hiking into my old age. ~ Marlyn Doan

- Make your feet your friend. ~ J.M. Barrie

- I haven't got any special religion this morning. My god is the God of walkers. If you walk hard enough, you probably don't need any other god. ~ Bruce Chatwin

- Jogging is for people who aren't intelligent enough to watch television.
  ~ Victoria Wood

- I only went out for a walk and finally concluded to stay out till sundown, for going out, I found, was really going in. ~ John Muir

- There is nothing like walking to get the feel of a country. A fine landscape is like a piece of music; it must be taken at the right tempo. Even a bicycle goes too fast. ~ Paul Scott Mowrer

- I represent what is left of a vanishing race, and that is the pedestrian... That I am still able to be here, I owe to a keen eye and a nimble pair of legs. But I know they'll get me someday. ~ Will Rogers

- I, who cannot stay in my chamber for a single day without acquiring some rust, and when sometimes I have stolen forth for a walk at the eleventh hour of four o'clock in the afternoon, too late to redeem the day, when the shades of night were already beginning to be mingled with the daylight, have felt as if I had committed some sin to be atoned for. ~ Thoreau

- Perhaps the truth depends on a walk around the lake. ~ Wallace Stevens

- If you are seeking creative ideas, go out walking. Angels whisper to a man when he goes for a walk. ~ Raymond Inmon

- I think that I cannot preserve my health and spirits, unless I spend four hours a day at least—and it is commonly more than that—sauntering through the woods and over the hills and fields, absolutely free from all worldly engagements. ~ Thoreau

- If you are walking to seek, ye shall find. ~ Sommeil Liberosensa

- Most men take the straight and narrow. A few take the road less traveled. I chose to cut through the woods. ~ Unknown

- If you want to forget all your other troubles, wear too tight shoes. ~ The Houghton Line

- I'm the walkingest girl around. I like to work at it—really get my heart pounding. ~ Amy Yasbeck

- I believe that the good Lord gave us a finite number of heartbeats and I'm damned if I'm going to use up mine running up and down a street. ~ Neil Armstrong

- In the morning a man walks with his whole body; in the evening, only with his legs. ~ Ralph Waldo Emerson

- It's not about winning, it's about finishing!

- I don't jog. If I die, I want to be sick. ~ Abe Lemmons

- The Americans never walk. In winter too cold and in summer too hot. ~ J.B. Yeats

- Jogging is very beneficial. It's good for your legs and your feet. It's also very good for the ground. It makes it feel needed.
  ~ Charles M. Shultz

- The difference between a jogger and a runner is an entry blank. ~ George Sheehan

- My grandmother started walking five miles a day when she was sixty. She's ninety—three today and we don't know where the hell she is. ~ Ellen Degeneres

- Nothing like a nighttime stroll to give you ideas.
  ~ J.K. Rowling

- Real athletes run, others just play games. ~ Solvitur ambulando,

- To solve a problem, walk around." ~ Gregory Mcnamee

- The civilized man has built a coach, but has lost the use of his feet.
  ~ Ralph Waldo Emerson

- If you pick 'em up, O Lord, I'll put 'em down.
  ~ "Prayer of the Tired Walker"

- The night walked down the sky with the moon in her hand. ~ Frederick L. Knowles

- My father considered a walk among the mountains as the equivalent of churchgoing. ~ Aldous Huxley

- The trouble with jogging is that the ice falls out of your glass. ~ Martin Mull

- Methinks that the moment my legs begin to move, my thoughts begin to flow. ~ Thoreau

- The true charm of pedestrianism does not lie in the walking or in the scenery, but in the talking. The walking is good to time the movement of the tongue by and to keep the blood and the brain stirred up and active; the scenery and the woodsy smells are good to bear in upon a man an unconscious and unobtrusive charm and solace to eye and soul and sense; but the supreme pleasure comes from the talk. ~ Mark Twain

- We live in a fast-paced society. Walking slows us down. ~ Robert Sweetgall

- There is nothing like walking to get the feel of a country. A fine landscape is like a piece of music; it must be taken at the right tempo. Even a bicycle goes too fast. ~ Paul Scott Mowrer

- Your body is built for walking. ~ Gary Yanker

- There is this to be said for walking: it's the one mode of human locomotion by which a man proceeds on his own two feet, upright, erect, as a man should be, not squatting on his rear haunches like a frog. ~ Edward Abbey

- Walking gets the feet moving, the blood moving, the mind moving. And movement is life. ~ Carrie Latet

- Human dignity insisted on the right to walk, a rhythm not extorted from the body by command or terror. The walk, the stroll, were private ways of passing time, the heritage of the feudal promenade in the nineteenth century. ~ Theodor W. Adorno

- Walking is good for solving problems—it's like the feet are little psychiatrists. ~ Pepper Giardino

- Walking isn't a lost art—one must, by some means, get to the garage. ~ Evan Esar

- Walks. The body advances, while the mind flutters around it like a bird. ~ Jules Renard

- What really helps motivate me to walk are my dogs, who are my best pals. They keep you honest about walking because when it's time to go, you can't disappoint those little faces. ~ Wendie Malick

- Walking takes longer than any other known form of locomotion except crawling. Thus it stretches time and prolongs life. Life is already too short to waste on speed. ~ Edward Abbey

- Thoughts come clearly while one walks. ~ Thomas Mann

- It is not talking but walking that will bring us to heaven. ~ Matthew Henry

- When you have worn out your shoes, the strength of the shoe leather has passed into the fiber of your body. I measure your health by the number of shoes and hats and clothes you have worn out. ~ Ralph Waldo Emerson

- You need special shoes for hiking—and a bit of a special soul as well.
  ~ Emme Woodhull-Bäche
- All truly great thoughts are conceived by walking.
  ~ Nietzsche

Water Polo

- All Wet
- Dive Right In
- Instant Polo Player: Just Add Water
- No "Marco"— Just POLO!
- Polo Pirate
- Splash!
- Splash Dance
- A Splashing Good Time
- Water Wars
- Wet and Wild
- I didn't know one thing about the sport. I used to wonder how they got the horses in the pool.
  ~ Dick Enberg, on his first water polo match TV assignment
- Water Polo: If it was easy, they'd call it "swimming."
- Water polo: the stamina of a marathon, the contact of hockey, the strategy of chess. ~ T-shirt

- Water polo players have a lot going on beneath the surface.
- I want to play Division I water polo. I don't really like swimming. It's kind of boring. ~ Kelly Eaton

Wrestling

- And in This Corner...
- Attitude is Everything
- Can't Hold Me Down
- Clinching the Deal
- Do You Prefer Push or Safety?
- Down for the Count
- Eating Mat
- Face to Face
- Get Ready to Rumble
- Go to the Mat
- Grappling Giants
- Hold Me Close
- King of the Mat
- Mat Mates
- Miracle on the Mat
- No Holds Barred
- On the Mat
- Ready to Rumble!
- Take Down

- Taking It to the Mat
- That Clinches It
- The Winner, and Still Cham-Pe-En...
- Wrestle Mania
- You're About to Get Pinned!
- Wrestling has been a way of life with me day in and day out. I won't get too far away from it. I might walk through the wrestling room once a week. I could go every day if I wanted. But just walk through, make sure it's still there. ~ Dan Gable
- I swear it upon Zeus an outstanding runner cannot be the equal of an average wrestler. ~ Socrates
- I hate questioning, but I love wrestling. ~ Aaron Smith
- There's no drama like wrestling. ~ Andy Kaufman
- More enduringly than any other sport, wrestling teaches self-control and pride. Some have wrestled without great skill—none have wrestled without pride. ~ Dan Gable
- The art of living is more like wrestling than dancing. ~ Marcus Aurelius
- He who hesitates, meditates in a horizontal position. ~ Ed Parker
- No 1/2 time; no substitutions; no time outs; no excuses.
- Wrestling is ballet with violence. ~ Jesse Ventura
- Pain is the best instructor, but no one wants to go to his class. ~ Hong Hi Choi
- Life has meaning only in the struggle. ~ Swami Sivananda
- I wrestle with demons of doubt. With my past failures. With my injuries. With that unrelenting voice that tells me to stop. But I am a wrestler and one thing is certain. I will be victorious. ~ Unknown
- He who wrestles with us strengthens our nerves and sharpens our skill. Our antagonist is our helper. ~ Edmund Burke
- Strength does not come from winning. Your struggles develop your strengths. When you go through hardships and decide not to surrender, that is strength. ~ Arnold Schwarzenegger
- It's not the size of the dog, it is the size of the fight in the dog. ~ Proverb

My Own **Sporty** Quotes

My Own Sporty Quotes

MY OWN SPORTY QUOTES

MY OWN SPORTY QUOTES

MY OWN SPORTY QUOTES

About the Author

Jennifer Smith, a scrapbooker and the devoted mother of two sons, loves to create scrapbook layouts focusing on the talents of her two aspiring athletes. With so many sporting event photos, she noticed the titles of her pages began to sound the same. In her search for inspiration, Smith found nothing solely sports related. She thought, "If I am looking for this, others who scrapbook may need it too."

This is Jennifer's first book. She hopes you will find it the winning solution to scrapbooking your family's memories of those gold-medal sporting events.

OUR BEST SELLERS

Ultimate Guide to the Perfect Word
Sold over 216,000 copies—352 pages

Ultimate Card—2nd Edition
Verses for Every Occasion

Ultimate Kids (Birth—Preschool)
Ultimate Kids II (K—6th Grade)
The Ultimate Kids Collection

Where's Thena? I need a poem about...
Best-Selling Poet Laureate of the Message Boards

Whispers
It's All About Love

What Can I Say?
Poetic Word-art

BoardSmartz and Taste of Paste
A Delightful Duo for Teachers and Educators

Letters to Heaven
Words of Comfort for the Grieving Soul

Color Made Easy
Misti Wrote the Book on Color!

C is for Christmas
Words to Decorate the Holidays

Military Moments
Words to Honor Our American Heroes

The Doodle Formula
Embellish Your Life: Learn the Art of Doodling!

Love Lines Word-art CD
Embellishments at the Click of a Mouse

Ultimate Sampler Word/Card CD
A Sampling of the Best Selling duo on CD

Ultimate Kids 1&2 Sampler
Quotes on CD Ready to Use

Clear Quotes
Word-art Transparencies

Brit Wit
Beautiful Full Color Transparencies

New Titles
Coming Soon!

Bluegrass Publishing, Inc.
Mayfield, KY 42066
(270) 251-3600
www.BluegrassPublishing.com

BLUEGRASS PUBLISHING, INC.
ORDER FORM

NAME	DATE
ADDRESS	
CITY/STATE	
CREDIT CARD #	EXP. DATE
PHONE ( ) —	
E-MAIL	

QTY	TITLE	EACH	TOTAL
	The Ultimate Guide to the Perfect Word BY LINDA LATOURELLE · OUR BIGGEST SELLER	$19.95	
	The Ultimate Guide to the Perfect Card BY LINDA LATOURELLE · NEW/BIGGER-384 PG	$19.95	
	The Ultimate Guide to Celebrating Kids I BY LINDA LATOURELLE · BIRTH TO PRESCHOOL	$19.95	
	The Ultimate Guide to Celebrating Kids II BY LINDA LATOURELLE · GRADE SCHOOL	$19.95	
	LoveLines CD—Beautifully designed quotes BY LINDA LATOURELLE · WORD-ART CD	$9.95	
	Military Moments BY THENA SMITH	$14.95	
	C is for Christmas with Bonus CD BY THENA SMITH	$14.95	
	Where's Thena? I need a poem about... BY THENA SMITH	$19.95	
	The Whole Megillah: Jewish scrapbooking BY CARLA BIRNBERG	$14.95	

SEND ORDER TO:
BLUEGRASS PUBLISHING, INC
PO BOX 634
MAYFIELD, KY 42066
(270) 251-3600
FAX (270) 251-3603
ORDERS@BLUEGRASSPUBLISHING.CO

6% TAX KENTUCKY	
$3.50 Per Book	Disc. Given on 3 or more
TOTAL AMOUNT	
$	